28th International Conference on Computational Linguistics (COLING 2020)

Tutorial Abstracts

Held online due to COVID-19

Barcelona, Spain
12 December 2020

ISBN: 978-1-7138-2524-1

Printed from e-media with permission by:

Curran Associates, Inc.
57 Morehouse Lane
Red Hook, NY 12571

Some format issues inherent in the e-media version may also appear in this print version.

Association for Computational Linguistics
209 N. Eighth Street
Stroudsburg, Pennsylvania 18360

Phone: 1-570-476-8006
Fax: 1-570-476-0860

acl@aclweb.org

Additional copies of this publication are available from:

Curran Associates, Inc.
57 Morehouse Lane
Red Hook, NY 12571 USA
Phone: 845-758-0400
Fax: 845-758-2633
Email: curran@proceedings.com
Web: www.proceedings.com

COLING 2020

The 28th International Conference on Computational Linguistics

Tutorial Abstracts

December 12th, 2020
Barcelona, Spain (Online)

Introduction

Welcome to the Tutorials Session of COLING 2020.

The COLING tutorials session is organised to give conference attendees a comprehensive introduction by expert researchers to some topics of importance drawn from our rapidly growing and changing research field.

This year, the call, submission, reviewing and selection of tutorials were coordinated jointly for multiple conferences: ACL, AACL-IJCNLP, COLING and EMNLP. We formed a review committee of 19 members, including the ACL tutorial chairs (Agata Savary and Yue Zhang), the EMNLP tutorial chairs (Benjamin van Durme and Aline Villavicencio), the COLING tutorial chairs (Daniel Beck and Lucia Specia), the AACL-IJCNMP tutorial chairs (Timothy Baldwin and Fei Xia) and 11 external reviewers (Emily Bender, Erik Cambria, Gaël Dias, Stefan Evert, Yang Liu, João Sedoc, Xu Sun, Yulia Tsvetkov, Taro Watanabe, Aaron Steven White and Meishan Zhang). Each proposal received at least three reviews, and the selection criteria included clarity, preparedness, novelty, timeliness, instructors' experience, likely audience, open access to the teaching materials, diversity (multilingualism, gender, age and geolocation) and the compatibility of preferred venues. A total of 43 tutorial submissions were received, of which seven were selected for presentation at COLING.

We solicited two types of tutorials to cover cutting-edge themes as well as introductory themes. The seven tutorials selected for COLING include three introductory and four cutting-edge topics. The introductory tutorials are dedicated to cross-lingual semantic representations, grammatical error correction and embeddings for NLP. The cutting-edge tutorials address the topics of multilingual neural machine translation, detection of rumours and misinformation, modelling of endangered languages and novel datasets for question answering, natural language inference and commonsense reasoning.

We would like to thank the tutorial authors for their contributions and flexibility while organising the conference virtually. We are also grateful to the 11 external reviewers for their valuable help in the decision process. Finally, our thanks go to the conference organisers for effective collaboration, and in particular to the general chair Donia Scott and the website chairs Laura Pérez-Mayos and Amita Misra.

We hope you enjoy the tutorials.

COLING 2020 Tutorial Co-chairs
Lucia Specia
Daniel Beck

Table of Contents

Tutorial at COLING 2020
Cross-lingual Semantic Representation for NLP with UCCA

Omri Abend[*], **Dotan Dvir**[*], **Daniel Hershcovich**[**],
Jakob Prange[***], and **Nathan Schneider**[***]

[*]Hebrew University of Jerusalem
[**]University of Copenhagen
[***]Georgetown University
oabend@cs.huji.ac.il, dotan.dvir@mail.huji.ac.il, dh@di.ku.dk
jakob@cs.georgetown.edu, nathan.schneider@georgetown.edu

Abstract

This is an introductory tutorial to UCCA (Universal Conceptual Cognitive Annotation), a cross-linguistically applicable framework for semantic representation, with corpora annotated in English, German and French, and ongoing annotation in Russian and Hebrew. UCCA builds on extensive typological work and supports rapid annotation. The tutorial will provide a detailed introduction to the UCCA annotation guidelines, design philosophy and the available resources; and a comparison to other meaning representations. It will also survey the existing parsing work, including the findings of three recent shared tasks, in SemEval and CoNLL, that addressed UCCA parsing. Finally, the tutorial will present recent applications and extensions to the scheme, demonstrating its value for natural language processing in a range of languages and domains.

1 Introduction

Universal Conceptual Cognitive Annotation (Abend and Rappoport, 2013), abbreviated as "UCCA", is a symbolic meaning representation (MR) that supports human annotation of text with broad coverage. While several meaning representation schemes share this goal (Abend and Rappoport, 2017), UCCA targets a level of semantic granularity that abstracts away from syntactic paraphrases in a typologically-motivated, cross-linguistic fashion, building on Basic Linguistic Theory (Dixon, 20102012), an influential framework for linguistic description. The scheme does not rely on language-specific resources, and sets a low threshold for annotator training.

UCCA has been annotated on several corpora of different genres and languages,[1] as summarized in table 1. Pilot studies have been conducted in additional languages. A web-based annotation system is available (Abend et al., 2017).

In UCCA, an analysis of a text passage is a directed acyclic graph over semantic elements called *units*. The principal kind of unit is a *scene*, which describes an action, movement or state, and is similar to FrameNet's notion of a *frame*. Figure 1 contains three scenes, evoked, respectively, by the verb *took*, the noun phrase *a repair*, and the possessive *our*. Several elements are exemplified, including participants, secondary relations, and scene linkage. The graph is anchored in the text tokens (the leaves generally correspond to one or more tokens), and relations between units are indicated by the *categories* assigned to the edges connecting them.

The goals of this tutorial are: to describe the UCCA representation as a linguistic scheme and how it is being used computationally, especially for cross-lingual and multilingual NLP; to familiarize participants with existing UCCA parsers and equip them with the conceptual tools required for desigining new parsers; and to review existing extensions and possible future directions.[2]

2 Relevance

UCCA resources and applications are valuable for cross-lingual NLP: like Universal Dependencies (Nivre et al., 2020), UCCA's category set can in principle be applied to a wide variety of languages.

[1]https://github.com/UniversalConceptualCognitiveAnnotation

[2]All material is available at http://bit.ly/ucca-tutorial.

Proceedings of the 28th International Conference on Computational Linguistics: Tutorial Abstracts, pages 1–9
Barcelona, Spain (Online), December 12th, 2020.

	Genre	# Tokens	# Sentences
English			
Wiki	Encyclopedia	158,573	5,141
20k	Literary	12,574	492
EWT	Online reviews	55,590	3,813
WSJ	Financial news	2,273	100
LPP	Literary	1,322	100
German			
20k	Literary	144,531	6,510
LPP	Literary	18,653	1,042
French			
20k	Literary	12,954	492
Hebrew, Russian			
LPP	Literary	annotation underway	

Table 1: Data statistics for existing UCCA corpora.

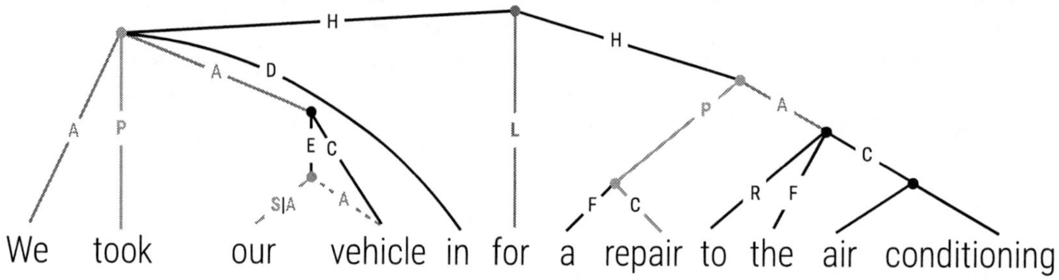

Figure 1: Example sentence from EWT (`reviews-086839-0003`), with its UCCA annotation. Category abbreviations: **H** = parallel scene, **L** = scene linker, **P** = process (dynamic event), **S** = state, **A** = scene participant, **D** = scene adverbial, **E** = non-scene elaborator, **C** = center (non-scene head), **R** = relator, **F** = functional element.

It is also cross-linguistically stable, and reflects a level of semantic structure that is usually preserved in translations (Sulem et al., 2015). UCCA has been applied in NLP to text simplification (Sulem et al., 2018b; Sulem et al., 2020), and text-to-text generation evaluation (Birch et al., 2016; Mareček et al., 2017; Choshen and Abend, 2018; Sulem et al., 2018b; Alva-Manchego et al., 2019; Xu et al., 2020). The tutorial will describe the guidelines and rationale behind UCCA, helping potential application designers understand what abstractions it makes.

Significant effort has been devoted to building UCCA parsers (Hershcovich et al., 2017; Hershcovich et al., 2018; Jiang et al., 2019; Lyu et al., 2019; Tuan Nguyen and Tran, 2019; Taslimipoor et al., 2019; Marzinotto et al., 2019; Pütz and Glocker, 2019; Yu and Sagae, 2019; Zhang et al., 2019a; Hershcovich and Arviv, 2019; Li et al., 2019; Donatelli et al., 2019; Che et al., 2019; Bai and Zhao, 2019; Lai et al., 2019; Koreeda et al., 2019; Straka and Straková, 2019; Cao et al., 2019; Zhang et al., 2019b; Droganova et al., 2019; Chen et al., 2019; Arviv et al., 2020; Samuel and Straka, 2020; Dou et al., 2020), including a SemEval 2019 shared task on cross-lingual UCCA parsing (Hershcovich et al., 2019b), which had 8 participating teams, as well as CoNLL 2019 and CoNLL 2020 shared tasks on cross-framework and cross-lingual meaning representation parsing (Oepen et al., 2019; Oepen et al., 2020), where 12 and 4 teams, respectively, submitted parsed UCCA graphs. This tutorial will allow researchers interested in UCCA parsing, and more generally graph parsing, deepen their understanding of the framework, and what properties make it unique. The tutorial will include a brief survey of the various approaches taken by existing parsers, and prepare attendees to work on UCCA parsing themselves.

Furthermore, UCCA parsing has been shown to benefit from multi-task learning (Caruana, 1997) with other meaning representations (Hershcovich et al., 2018), although results from the CoNLL 2019 and CoNLL 2020 shared tasks (Oepen et al., 2019; Oepen et al., 2020) show that multi-task meaning representation parsing is difficult. The tutorial will compare and contrast UCCA and other meaning representations, and will thereby inform participants of the potential advantages and difficulties in employing multi-task learning across semantic schemes.

UCCA defines a small inventory of coarse-grained categories so as not to rely on language-specific lexical resources, and can thus in principle be applied to a great variety of languages. This distinguishes UCCA from finer-grained sentence-structural representations like FrameNet (Baker et al., 1998), the Abstract Meaning Representation (Banarescu et al., 2013), which relies on PropBank (Palmer et al., 2005), and Universal Decompositional Semantics (White et al., 2016). For example, FrameNet requires a different ontology for each new language addressed (Ohara et al., 2003; You and Liu, 2005; Borin et al., 2013; Park et al., 2014; Hayoun and Elhadad, 2016; Djemaa et al., 2016), and AMR underwent significant customization to be applicable to Chinese (Li et al., 2016). Decomp takes a different approach to multilinguality, where the parser is required to parse sentences in other languages to their corresponding *English* semantic forms (Zhang et al., 2018). The tutorial will address contemporary issues in the field, such as the question of how to represent semantic structure multilingually with broad coverage, which is actively being explored from many angles.

While UCCA structures and categories are intentionally coarse, the scheme has a multi-layered architecture, which allows for refinement using additional *layers*, which serve as "modules" of semantic distinctions. We will give an overview of the recently proposed extensions (to support coreference) and joint parsing experiments (Prange et al., 2019a; Prange et al., 2019b).

3 Agenda

The planned division of time is as follows:

1. **Bird's eye view (45m).** Design philosophy, notion of scenes, basic explanation of categories, simple examples.

2. **Annotation guidelines (35m).** Linguistic details, interesting constructions in several languages.

3. **Data and annotation (10m).** Overview of annotated data (see §1) and the annotation process and software (Abend et al., 2017).

4. **Extensions to UCCA and integration with other schemes (15m).** Semantic roles (Prange et al., 2019a), coreference (Prange et al., 2019b), and fine-grained implicit arguments (Cui and Hershcovich, 2020).

5. **Relation to other representations (15m).** Comparison to other meaning representations (Abend and Rappoport, 2017; Koller et al., 2019; Hershcovich et al., 2020) and to UD (Hershcovich et al., 2019a).

6. **Parsing (25m).** TUPA (Hershcovich et al., 2017; Hershcovich et al., 2018; Hershcovich and Arviv, 2019; Arviv et al., 2020), SemEval 2019 Task 1 (Hershcovich et al., 2019b; Jiang et al., 2019), CoNLL 2019 and CoNLL 2020 Shared Tasks (Oepen et al., 2019; Oepen et al., 2020), and more recent parsers (Zhang et al., 2019a).

7. **Monolingual tasks and evaluation (20m).** Sentence simplification (Sulem et al., 2018b), evaluation of sentence simplification (Sulem et al., 2018a; Alva-Manchego et al., 2019) and grammatical error correction (Choshen and Abend, 2018).

8. **Cross-linguistic studies and applications (15m).** Analysis of cross-linguistic stability (Sulem et al., 2015), machine translation evaluation (Birch et al., 2016; Mareček et al., 2017; Xu et al., 2020) and simplification for machine translation (Sulem et al., 2020).

3.1 Prerequisites

No prior knowledge is assumed about linguistics and typology. The necessary background will be provided as part of the tutorial. However, participants are expected to know about basic data structures such as trees and graphs. For the parsing section, prior knowledge is assumed about common machine learning techniques, including supervised learning and neural networks.

3.2 Reading list

The following are recommended to read before the tutorial, as they provide background and frame the context in which the tutorial materials lie:

1. Chapter 3 of Dixon (2005) contains an introduction to some basic concepts in semantics on which UCCA is based.

2. Kiperwasser and Goldberg (2016) present a transition-based parser using an architecture on which TUPA, the first UCCA parser, is based (Hershcovich et al., 2017).

3. Peng et al. (2017) performed multi-task learning for meaning representation parsing, inspiring work on cross-framework parsing for UCCA (Hershcovich et al., 2018).

4. Abend and Rappoport (2017) compare and constrast several meaning representations according to various aspects.

5. Deng and Xue (2017) investigate translation divergences using a hierarchical alignment, and discuss bridging them with cross-lingual semantic representations.

6. Croft et al. (2017) list typologically-informed design criteria for Universal Dependencies (Nivre et al., 2020), which are also relevant for other structural representations in NLP.

4 Presenters

The instruction in this tutorial involves organizers at various career stages, exhibiting geographic diversity, and diversity in terms of gender.

Omri Abend (`https://www.cse.huji.ac.il/~oabend`) is a Senior Lecturer (Assistant Professor) of Computer Science and Cognitive Science at the Hebrew University of Jerusalem. Research interests: computational semantics and specifically, cross-linguistically applicable semantic and grammatical representation, semantic parsing, corpus annotation and evaluation. Relevant experience: co-developer of the UCCA scheme, partner in all annotation and application efforts related to UCCA, and in some of the parsing efforts. Publishes regularly in NLP conferences (ACL, NAACL, EMNLP etc.).

Dotan Dvir has been managing the UCCA manual annotation project at the Hebrew University of Jerusalem since 2017. She was involved in writing version 2 of the UCCA guidelines. She has in-depth knowledge of the UCCA guidelines and is experienced in instructing annotators about them. Before joining the UCCA project, she had been working as a text analyst in IBM's Project Debater (2014-2017).

Daniel Hershcovich (`https://danielhers.github.io`) is a Tenure-Track Assistant Professor at the University of Copenhagen, Denmark. Daniel pioneered the work on UCCA parsing, and is interested in semantic parsing and meaning representations. Daniel develops and maintains the UCCA toolkit Python codebase,[3] has teaching experience in NLP and ML courses, and publishes in NLP conferences.

Jakob Prange (`https://prange.jakob.georgetown.domains`) is pursuing his Ph.D. at Georgetown University, investigating design, annotation, and parsing strategies for various meaning representations. Among other formalisms (SNACS, frame semantics, STAG, CCG), he has studied and worked with UCCA over the past two years, which recently resulted in two published proposals of novel

[3] `https://github.com/danielhers/ucca`

UCCA extensions, for coreference and semantic roles. He has experience with teaching in multicultural classroom settings and presenting research at international conferences.

Nathan Schneider (http://nathan.cl) leads an interdisciplinary computational linguistics research group at Georgetown University. He has worked on the design and parsing of a range of broad-coverage representations for different aspects and granularities of meaning, including multiword expressions, supersenses, frame semantics, AMR, and UCCA (as a multiyear collaboration with the copresenters). He has experience teaching meaning representations in classroom settings as well as conference tutorials—notably, a tutorial on AMR (Schneider et al., 2015) whose materials[4] continue to serve as a useful introduction to the scheme, and will serve as a model for the proposed UCCA tutorial.

References

Omri Abend and Ari Rappoport. 2013. Universal Conceptual Cognitive Annotation (UCCA). In *Proc. of ACL*, pages 228–238, August.

Omri Abend and Ari Rappoport. 2017. The state of the art in semantic representation. In *Proc. of ACL*, pages 77–89.

Omri Abend, Shai Yerushalmi, and Ari Rappoport. 2017. UCCAApp: Web-application for syntactic and semantic phrase-based annotation. *Proc. of ACL System Demonstrations*, pages 109–114.

Fernando Alva-Manchego, Louis Martin, Carolina Scarton, and Lucia Specia. 2019. EASSE: Easier Automatic Sentence Simplification Evaluation. In *To Appear in EMNLP-ICJNLP 2019: System Demonstrations*, Hong Kong, China, November.

Ofir Arviv, Ruixiang Cui, and Daniel Hershcovich. 2020. HUJI-KU at MRP 2020: Two transition-based neural parsers. In *Proceedings of the CoNLL 2020 Shared Task: Cross-Framework Meaning Representation Parsing*, pages 73 – 82, Online.

Hongxiao Bai and Hai Zhao. 2019. SJTU at MRP 2019: A transition-based multi-task parser for cross-framework meaning representation parsing. In *Proceedings of the Shared Task on Cross-Framework Meaning Representation Parsing at the 2019 Conference on Computational Natural Language Learning*, pages 86 – 94, Hong Kong, China.

Collin F. Baker, Charles J. Fillmore, and John B. Lowe. 1998. The Berkeley FrameNet project. In *ACL-COLING '98*.

Laura Banarescu, Claire Bonial, Shu Cai, Madalina Georgescu, Kira Griffitt, Ulf Hermjakob, Kevin Knight, Martha Palmer, and Nathan Schneider. 2013. Abstract Meaning Representation for sembanking. In *Proc. of the Linguistic Annotation Workshop*.

Alexandra Birch, Omri Abend, Ondřej Bojar, and Barry Haddow. 2016. HUME: Human UCCA-based evaluation of machine translation. In *Proceedings of the 2016 Conference on Empirical Methods in Natural Language Processing*, pages 1264–1274, Austin, Texas, November. Association for Computational Linguistics.

Lars Borin, Markus Forsberg, and Benjamin Lyngfelt. 2013. 2) close encounters of the fifth kind: Some linguistic and computational aspects of the Swedish FrameNet++ project. *Veredas-Revista de Estudos Linguísticos*, 17(1-).

Jie Cao, Yi Zhang, Adel Youssef, and Vivek Srikumar. 2019. Amazon at MRP 2019: Parsing meaning representations with lexical and phrasal anchoring. In *Proceedings of the Shared Task on Cross-Framework Meaning Representation Parsing at the 2019 Conference on Computational Natural Language Learning*, pages 138 – 148, Hong Kong, China.

Rich Caruana. 1997. Multitask Learning. *Machine Learning*, 28(1):41–75, jul.

Wanxiang Che, Longxu Dou, Yang Xu, Yuxuan Wang, Yijia Liu, and Ting Liu. 2019. HIT-SCIR at MRP 2019: A unified pipeline for meaning representation parsing via efficient training and effective encoding. In *Proceedings of the Shared Task on Cross-Framework Meaning Representation Parsing at the 2019 Conference on Computational Natural Language Learning*, pages 76 – 85, Hong Kong, China.

[4]https://github.com/nschneid/amr-tutorial/

Yufei Chen, Yajie Ye, and Weiwei Sun. 2019. Peking at MRP 2019: Factorization- and composition-based parsing for Elementary Dependency Structures. In *Proceedings of the Shared Task on Cross-Framework Meaning Representation Parsing at the 2019 Conference on Computational Natural Language Learning*, pages 166 – 176, Hong Kong, China.

Leshem Choshen and Omri Abend. 2018. Automatic metric validation for grammatical error correction. In *Proceedings of the 56th Annual Meeting of the Association for Computational Linguistics (Volume 1: Long Papers)*, pages 1372–1382, Melbourne, Australia, July. Association for Computational Linguistics.

William Croft, Dawn Nordquist, Katherine Looney, and Michael Regan. 2017. Linguistic typology meets universal dependencies. In *TLT*, pages 63–75.

Ruixiang Cui and Daniel Hershcovich. 2020. Refining implicit argument annotation for UCCA. In *Proc. of DMR*.

Dun Deng and Nianwen Xue. 2017. Translation divergences in chinese–english machine translation: An empirical investigation. *Computational Linguistics*, 43(3):521–565.

R.M.W. Dixon. 2005. *A Semantic Approach to English Grammar*. Oxford University Press, Oxford.

Robert M. W. Dixon. 2010/2012. *Basic Linguistic Theory*. Oxford University Press.

Marianne Djemaa, Marie Candito, Philippe Muller, and Laure Vieu. 2016. Corpus annotation within the French FrameNet: a domain-by-domain methodology. In *Proceedings of the Tenth International Conference on Language Resources and Evaluation (LREC'16)*, pages 3794–3801, Portorož, Slovenia, May. European Language Resources Association (ELRA).

Lucia Donatelli, Meaghan Fowlie, Jonas Groschwitz, Alexander Koller, Matthias Lindemann, Mario Mina, and Pia WeiSSenhorn. 2019. Saarland at MRP 2019: Compositional parsing across all graphbanks. In *Proceedings of the Shared Task on Cross-Framework Meaning Representation Parsing at the 2019 Conference on Computational Natural Language Learning*, pages 66 – 75, Hong Kong, China.

Longxu Dou, Yunlong Feng, Yuqiu Ji, Wanxiang Che, and Ting Liu. 2020. HIT-SCIR at MRP 2020: Transition-based parser and iterative inference parser. In *Proceedings of the CoNLL 2020 Shared Task: Cross-Framework Meaning Representation Parsing*, pages 65 – 72, Online.

Kira Droganova, Andrey Kutuzov, Nikita Mediankin, and Daniel Zeman. 2019. ÚFAL–Oslo at MRP 2019: Garage sale semantic parsing. In *Proceedings of the Shared Task on Cross-Framework Meaning Representation Parsing at the 2019 Conference on Computational Natural Language Learning*, pages 158 – 165, Hong Kong, China.

Avi Hayoun and Michael Elhadad. 2016. The Hebrew FrameNet project. In *Proceedings of the Tenth International Conference on Language Resources and Evaluation (LREC'16)*, pages 4341–4347, Portorož, Slovenia, May. European Language Resources Association (ELRA).

Daniel Hershcovich and Ofir Arviv. 2019. TUPA at MRP 2019: A multi-task baseline system. In *Proceedings of the Shared Task on Cross-Framework Meaning Representation Parsing at the 2019 Conference on Computational Natural Language Learning*, pages 28 – 39, Hong Kong, China.

Daniel Hershcovich, Omri Abend, and Ari Rappoport. 2017. A transition-based directed acyclic graph parser for UCCA. In *Proc. of ACL*, pages 1127–1138.

Daniel Hershcovich, Omri Abend, and Ari Rappoport. 2018. Multitask parsing across semantic representations. In *Proc. of ACL*, pages 373–385.

Daniel Hershcovich, Omri Abend, and Ari Rappoport. 2019a. Content differences in syntactic and semantic representation. In *Proc. of NAACL-HLT*.

Daniel Hershcovich, Leshem Choshen, Elior Sulem, Zohar Aizenbud, Ari Rappoport, and Omri Abend. 2019b. SemEval 2019 task 1: Cross-lingual semantic parsing with UCCA. In *Proc. of SemEval*.

Daniel Hershcovich, Nathan Schneider, Dotan Dvir, Jakob Prange, Miryam de Lhoneux, and Omri Abend. 2020. Comparison by conversion: Reverse-engineering UCCA from syntax and lexical semantics. In *Proc. of COLING*.

Wei Jiang, Zhenghua Li, Yu Zhang, and Min Zhang. 2019. HLT@SUDA at SemEval-2019 Task 1: UCCA graph parsing as constituent tree parsing. In *Proc. of SemEval*, pages 11–15, Minneapolis, Minnesota, USA, June.

Eliyahu Kiperwasser and Yoav Goldberg. 2016. Simple and accurate dependency parsing using bidirectional LSTM feature representations. *Transactions of the Association for Computational Linguistics*, 4:313–327.

Alexander Koller, Stephan Oepen, and Weiwei Sun. 2019. Graph-based meaning representations: Design and processing. In *Proceedings of the 57th Annual Meeting of the Association for Computational Linguistics: Tutorial Abstracts*, pages 6–11, Florence, Italy, July. Association for Computational Linguistics.

Yuta Koreeda, Gaku Morio, Terufumi Morishita, Hiroaki Ozaki, and Kohsuke Yanai. 2019. Hitachi at MRP 2019: Unified encoder-to-biaffine network for cross-framework meaning representation parsing. In *Proceedings of the Shared Task on Cross-Framework Meaning Representation Parsing at the 2019 Conference on Computational Natural Language Learning*, pages 114 – 126, Hong Kong, China.

Sunny Lai, Chun Hei Lo, Kwong Sak Leung, and Yee Leung. 2019. CUHK at MRP 2019: Transition-based parser with cross-framework variable-arity resolve action. In *Proceedings of the Shared Task on Cross-Framework Meaning Representation Parsing at the 2019 Conference on Computational Natural Language Learning*, pages 104 – 113, Hong Kong, China.

Bin Li, Yuan Wen, Weiguang Qu, Lijun Bu, and Nianwen Xue. 2016. Annotating the little prince with Chinese AMRs. In *Proceedings of the 10th Linguistic Annotation Workshop held in conjunction with ACL 2016 (LAW-X 2016)*, pages 7–15, Berlin, Germany, August. Association for Computational Linguistics.

Zuchao Li, Hai Zhao, Zhuosheng Zhang, Rui Wang, Masao Utiyama, and Eiichiro Sumita. 2019. SJTU–NICT at MRP 2019: Multi-task learning for end-to-end uniform semantic graph parsing. In *Proceedings of the Shared Task on Cross-Framework Meaning Representation Parsing at the 2019 Conference on Computational Natural Language Learning*, pages 45 – 54, Hong Kong, China.

Weimin Lyu, Sheng Huang, Abdul Rafae Khan, Shengqiang Zhang, Weiwei Sun, and Jia Xu. 2019. CUNY-PKU parser at SemEval-2019 task 1: Cross-lingual semantic parsing with UCCA. In *Proceedings of the 13th International Workshop on Semantic Evaluation*, pages 92–96, Minneapolis, Minnesota, USA, June. Association for Computational Linguistics.

David Mareček, Ondřej Bojar, Ondřej Hübsch, Rudolf Rosa, and Dušan Variš. 2017. CUNI experiments for WMT17 metrics task. In *Proceedings of the Second Conference on Machine Translation*, pages 604–611, Copenhagen, Denmark, September. Association for Computational Linguistics.

Gabriel Marzinotto, Johannes Heinecke, and Géraldine Damnati. 2019. MaskParse@deskin at SemEval-2019 task 1: Cross-lingual UCCA semantic parsing using recursive masked sequence tagging. In *Proceedings of the 13th International Workshop on Semantic Evaluation*, pages 107–112, Minneapolis, Minnesota, USA, June. Association for Computational Linguistics.

Joakim Nivre, Marie-Catherine de Marneffe, Filip Ginter, Jan Hajič, Christopher D. Manning, Sampo Pyysalo, Sebastian Schuster, Francis Tyers, and Daniel Zeman. 2020. Universal Dependencies v2: An evergrowing multilingual treebank collection. In *Proceedings of the 12th Language Resources and Evaluation Conference*, pages 4034–4043, Marseille, France, May. European Language Resources Association.

Stephan Oepen, Omri Abend, Jan Hajič, Daniel Hershcovich, Marco Kuhlmann, Tim O'Gorman, Nianwen Xue, Jayeol Chun, Milan Straka, and Zdeňka Urešová. 2019. MRP 2019: Cross-framework Meaning Representation Parsing. In *Proceedings of the Shared Task on Cross-Framework Meaning Representation Parsing at the 2019 Conference on Computational Natural Language Learning*, pages 1 – 27, Hong Kong, China.

Stephan Oepen, Omri Abend, Lasha Abzianidze, Johan Bos, Jan Hajič, Daniel Hershcovich, Bin Li, Tim O'Gorman, Nianwen Xue, and Daniel Zeman. 2020. MRP 2020: The Second Shared Task on Cross-framework and Cross-Lingual Meaning Representation Parsing. In *Proceedings of the CoNLL 2020 Shared Task: Cross-Framework Meaning Representation Parsing*, pages 1 – 22, Online.

Kyoko Hirose Ohara, Seiko Fujii, Hiroaki Saito, Shun Ishizaki, Toshio Ohori, and Ryoko Suzuki. 2003. The Japanese FrameNet project: A preliminary report. In *Proceedings of pacific association for computational linguistics*, pages 249–254. Citeseer.

Martha Palmer, Daniel Gildea, and Paul Kingsbury. 2005. The proposition bank: An annotated corpus of semantic roles. *Computational Linguistics*, 31(1).

Jungyeul Park, Sejin Nam, Youngsik Kim, Younggyun Hahm, Dosam Hwang, and Key-Sun Choi. 2014. Frame-semantic web: a case study for Korean. In *International Semantic Web Conference (Posters & Demos)*, pages 257–260.

Hao Peng, Sam Thomson, and Noah A. Smith. 2017. Deep multitask learning for semantic dependency parsing. In *Proc. of ACL*, pages 2037–2048.

Jakob Prange, Nathan Schneider, and Omri Abend. 2019a. Made for each other: Broad-coverage semantic structures meet preposition supersenses. In *Proc. of CoNLL*. To appear., November.

Jakob Prange, Nathan Schneider, and Omri Abend. 2019b. Semantically constrained multilayer annotation: The case of coreference. In *Proceedings of the First International Workshop on Designing Meaning Representations (DMR)*, pages 164–176, Florence, Italy, August. Association for Computational Linguistics.

Tobias Pütz and Kevin Glocker. 2019. Tüpa at SemEval-2019 task1: (almost) feature-free semantic parsing. In *Proceedings of the 13th International Workshop on Semantic Evaluation*, pages 113–118, Minneapolis, Minnesota, USA, June. Association for Computational Linguistics.

David Samuel and Milan Straka. 2020. ÚFAL at MRP 2020: Permutation-invariant semantic parsing in PERIN. In *Proceedings of the CoNLL 2020 Shared Task: Cross-Framework Meaning Representation Parsing*, pages 53 – 64, Online.

Nathan Schneider, Jeffrey Flanigan, and Tim O'Gorman. 2015. The logic of AMR: practical, unified, graph-based sentence semantics for NLP. In *Proc. of the 2015 Conference of the North American Chapter of the Association for Computational Linguistics: Tutorial Abstracts*, pages 4–5, Denver, Colorado, USA, May.

Milan Straka and Jana Straková. 2019. ÚFAL MRPipe at MRP 2019: UDPipe goes semantic in the Meaning Representation Parsing shared task. In *Proceedings of the Shared Task on Cross-Framework Meaning Representation Parsing at the 2019 Conference on Computational Natural Language Learning*, pages 127 – 137, Hong Kong, China.

Elior Sulem, Omri Abend, and Ari Rappoport. 2015. Conceptual annotations preserve structure across translations: A French-English case study. In *Proc. of S2MT*, pages 11–22.

Elior Sulem, Omri Abend, and Ari Rappoport. 2018a. Semantic structural evaluation for text simplification. In *Proceedings of the 2018 Conference of the North American Chapter of the Association for Computational Linguistics: Human Language Technologies, Volume 1 (Long Papers)*, pages 685–696, New Orleans, Louisiana, June. Association for Computational Linguistics.

Elior Sulem, Omri Abend, and Ari Rappoport. 2018b. Simple and effective text simplification using semantic and neural methods. In *Proceedings of the 56th Annual Meeting of the Association for Computational Linguistics (Volume 1: Long Papers)*, pages 162–173, Melbourne, Australia, July. Association for Computational Linguistics.

Elior Sulem, Omri Abend, and Ari Rappoport. 2020. Semantic structural decomposition for neural machine translation. In *Proc. of *SEM*.

Shiva Taslimipoor, Omid Rohanian, and Sara Može. 2019. GCN-sem at SemEval-2019 task 1: Semantic parsing using graph convolutional and recurrent neural networks. In *Proceedings of the 13th International Workshop on Semantic Evaluation*, pages 102–106, Minneapolis, Minnesota, USA, June. Association for Computational Linguistics.

Dang Tuan Nguyen and Trung Tran. 2019. DANGNT@UIT.VNU-HCM at SemEval 2019 task 1: Graph transformation system from Stanford basic dependencies to Universal Conceptual Cognitive Annotation (UCCA). In *Proceedings of the 13th International Workshop on Semantic Evaluation*, pages 97–101, Minneapolis, Minnesota, USA, June. Association for Computational Linguistics.

Aaron Steven White, Drew Reisinger, Keisuke Sakaguchi, Tim Vieira, Sheng Zhang, Rachel Rudinger, Kyle Rawlins, and Benjamin Van Durme. 2016. Universal decompositional semantics on Universal Dependencies. In *Proc. of EMNLP*, pages 1713–1723.

Jin Xu, Yinuo Guo, and Junfeng Hu. 2020. Incorporate semantic structures into machine translation evaluation via ucca.

Liping You and Kaiying Liu. 2005. Building Chinese FrameNet database. *2005 International Conference on Natural Language Processing and Knowledge Engineering*, pages 301–306.

Dian Yu and Kenji Sagae. 2019. UC Davis at SemEval-2019 task 1: DAG semantic parsing with attention-based decoder. In *Proceedings of the 13th International Workshop on Semantic Evaluation*, pages 119–124, Minneapolis, Minnesota, USA, June. Association for Computational Linguistics.

Sheng Zhang, Xutai Ma, Rachel Rudinger, Kevin Duh, and Benjamin Van Durme. 2018. Cross-lingual decompositional semantic parsing. In *Proceedings of the 2018 Conference on Empirical Methods in Natural Language Processing*, pages 1664–1675.

Sheng Zhang, Xutai Ma, Kevin Duh, and Benjamin Van Durme. 2019a. Broad-coverage semantic parsing as transduction. In *Proc. of EMNLP-IJCNLP*. To appear., November.

Yue Zhang, Wei Jiang, Qingrong Xia, Junjie Cao, Rui Wang, Zhenghua Li, and Min Zhang. 2019b. SUDA–Alibaba at MRP 2019: Graph-based models with BERT. In *Proceedings of the Shared Task on Cross-Framework Meaning Representation Parsing at the 2019 Conference on Computational Natural Language Learning*, pages 149 – 157, Hong Kong, China.

Embeddings in Natural Language Processing

Jose Camacho-Collados[1] and **Mohammad Taher Pilehvar**[2,3]
[1]School of Computer Science and Informatics, Cardiff University, UK
[2]Tehran Institute for Advanced Studies (TeIAS), Tehran, Iran
[3]DTAL, University of Cambridge, UK
camachocolladosj@cardiff.ac.uk, mp792@cam.ac.uk

Abstract

Embeddings have been one of the most important topics of interest in Natural Language Processing (NLP) for the past decade. Representing knowledge through a low-dimensional vector which is easily integrable in modern machine learning models has played a central role in the development of the field. Embedding techniques initially focused on words but the attention soon started to shift to other forms. This tutorial will provide a high-level synthesis of the main embedding techniques in NLP, in the broad sense. We will start by conventional word embeddings (e.g., Word2Vec and GloVe) and then move to other types of embeddings, such as sense-specific and graph alternatives. We will finalize with an overview of the trending contextualized representations (e.g., ELMo and BERT) and explain their potential and impact in NLP.

1 Description

In this tutorial we will start by providing a historical overview on word-level vector space models, and word embeddings in particular. Word embeddings (e.g. Word2Vec (Mikolov et al., 2013), GloVe (Pennington et al., 2014) or FastText (Bojanowski et al., 2017)) have proven to be powerful keepers of prior knowledge to be integrated into downstream Natural Language Processing (NLP) applications.

However, despite their flexibility and success in capturing semantic properties of words, the effectiveness of word embeddings are generally hampered by an important limitation, known as the meaning conflation deficiency: the inability to discriminate among different meanings of a word. A word can have one meaning (monosemous) or multiple meanings (ambiguous). For instance, the noun mouse can refer to two different meanings depending on the context: an animal or a computer device. Hence, mouse is said to be ambiguous. In fact, according to the Principle of Economical Versatility of Words (Zipf, 1949), frequent words tend to have more senses. Moreover, this meaning conflation can have additional negative impacts on accurate semantic modeling, e.g., semantically unrelated words that are similar to different senses of a word are pulled towards each other in the semantic space (Neelakantan et al., 2014; Pilehvar and Collier, 2016). In our example, the two semantically-unrelated words rat and screen are pulled towards each other in the semantic space for their similarities to two different senses of mouse (see Figure 1). This, in turn, contributes to the violation of the triangle inequality in euclidean spaces (Tversky and Gati, 1982; Neelakantan et al., 2014).

Accurately capturing the meaning of words (both ambiguous and unambiguous) plays a crucial role in the language understanding of NLP systems. In order to deal with the meaning conflation deficiency, this tutorial covers approaches have attempted to model individual word senses (Reisinger and Mooney, 2010; Huang et al., 2012; Neelakantan et al., 2014; Rothe and Schütze, 2015; Li and Jurafsky, 2015; Pilehvar and Collier, 2016; Mancini et al., 2017). Sense representation techniques, however, suffer from limitations which hinders their effective application in downstream NLP tasks: they either need vast amounts of training data to obtain reliable representations or require an additional sense disambiguation on the input text to make them integrable into NLP systems. This data is highly expensive to obtain in practice, which causes the so-called knowledge-acquisition bottleneck (Gale et al., 1992).

As a practical way to deal with the knowledge-acquisition bottleneck, an emerging branch of research has focused on directly integrating unsupervised embeddings into downstream models. Instead of learning a fixed number of senses per word, contextualized word embeddings learn "senses" dynamically,

Proceedings of the 28th International Conference on Computational Linguistics: Tutorial Abstracts, pages 10–15
Barcelona, Spain (Online), December 12th, 2020.

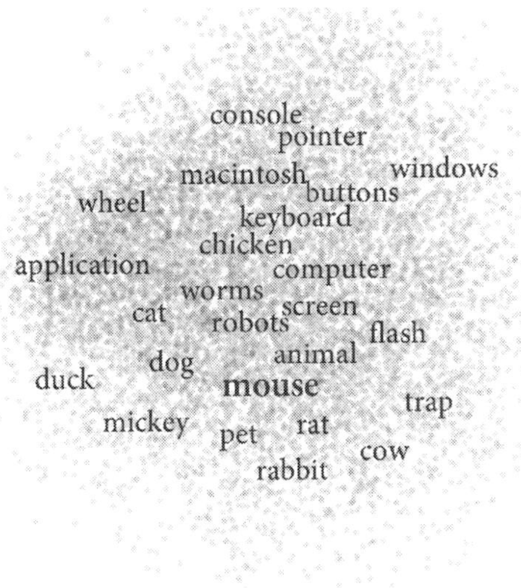

Figure 1: An illustration of the meaning conflation deficiency in a 2D semantic space around the ambiguous word *mouse*. Having the word, with its different meanings, represented as a single point (vector) results in pulling together of semantically unrelated words, such as *computer* and *rabbit*.

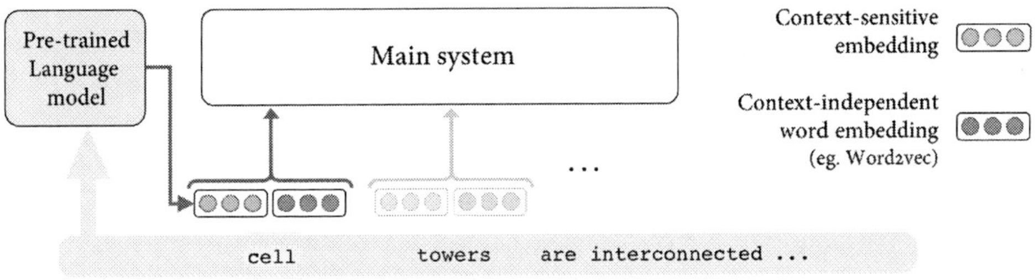

Figure 2: A general illustration of contextualized word embeddings and how they are integrated in NLP models. A language modelling component is responsible for analyzing the context of the target word (cell in the figure) and generating its dynamic embedding.

i.e., their representations dynamically change depending on the context in which a word appears. Context2vec (Melamud et al., 2016) and ELMo (Peters et al., 2018a) are some of the early examples for this type of representation. These models represent the context of a target word by extracting the embedding of a word in context from a bi-directional LSTM language model. The latter further proposed a seamless integration into neural NLP systems, as depicted in Figure 2. More recently, Transformers (Vaswani et al., 2017) have proven very effective for encoding contextualized knowledge, thanks to their self-attention mechanism (Figure 3). BERT (Devlin et al., 2018), which is based on Transformers, has revolutionized the field of representation learning and has impacted many other fields in NLP. Many derivatives and subsequent models have followed up, rapidly pushing up the state of the art in different benchmarks. In this tutorial we extensively cover this recent type of representation.

We also discuss other types of embeddings, for instance for graph structures which are a popular choice in many scenarios, or for longer units of texts such as sentences and documents. Finally, we conclude this tutorial by discussing some of the ethical issues around the implicit gender and stereotypical biases encoded in word embeddings and proposals for reducing these artifacts.

2 Type of tutorial

Cutting-edge, although the first part of the tutorial could also be considered introductory. The tutorial provides an overview starting from vector space models and word representations and the move to newer

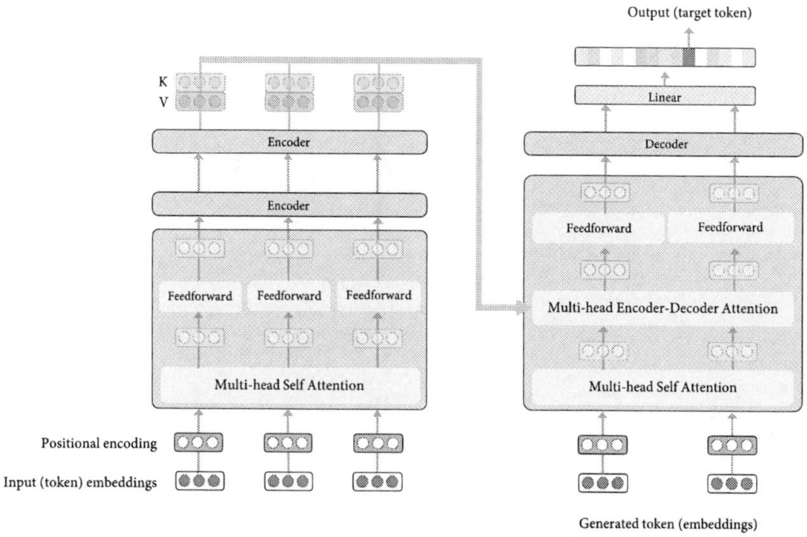

Figure 3: The overall structure of a Transformer-based encoder-decoder model. Many of the recent contextualised models, such as BERT, are based on Transformers.

contextualized embeddings.

3 Outline

The tutorial is split into seven sections, each of which being roughly self-contained.

1. Introduction (20 minutes) A quick warm-up introduction to NLP and why it is important for NLP systems to have a semantic comprehension of texts and how this is usually achieved by representing semantics through mathematical or computer-interpretable notations. This section provides necessary motivation for the tutorial and highlights the role of semantic representation as a core component of many NLP systems. It also briefly describes the Vector Space Model and briefly discusses the evolution path of semantic representations in NLP.

2. Word embeddings (25 minutes) This section explains the main approaches to learn word embeddings from text corpora, what their advantages are and how they have revolutionized the field of lexical semantics. We describe the concepts behind some of the major word embedding techniques, such as Word2vec and GloVe, and their application in NLP. Finally, we briefly cover other types of word embeddings, such as character-based, cross-lingual or knowledge-enhanced.

3. Graph Embeddings (20 minutes) Graphs are ubiquitous data structures. They are often the preferred choice for representing various type of data, including social networks, word co-occurrence and semantic networks, citation networks, telecommunication networks, molecular graph structures and biological networks. In this part of the tutorial, we discuss some of the prominent techniques for transforming graph nodes and edges into vectors. The goal is for the resulting embedding space to preserve the structural properties of the graph, be it the relative positioning of the nodes or relations (edges) among them.

4. Sense Embeddings (20 minutes) In this section we cover those approaches that learn distinct representations for individual meanings of words (i.e., word senses) with the aim of addressing the meaning conflation deficiency. For this part, we will discuss both knowledge-based and unsupervised paradigms.

5. Contextualized Representations (45 minutes) In this part of the tutorial we will introduce the latest type of embeddings that aim at providing dynamic representations of words, capable of adapting the representation to syntactic and semantic characteristics of a given context. We will start by discussing the need for contextualization. We then provide a very brief introduction to the architecture and building blocks of the Transformer model. We then start the overview of contextualized models by some of the earliest proposals in this category, i..e, Context2vec and "Embeddings from Language Models" (ELMo). We then discuss the newer and more prominent models based on Transformers. Specifically, we will describe BERT and some of its derivatives and subsequent works, such as XLNet, DistilBERT, GPT-2 and RoBERTa. We will provide an in-depth analysis of this techniques and point out not only their strengths, but also some of the limitations from which they suffer, which can be taken as possible research directions.

6. Sentence and Document Embeddings (15 minutes) This section goes beyond the level of words, and describes how sentences and documents can be encoded into vectorial representations. We cover some of the widely used supervised and unsupervised techniques and discuss the applications and evaluation methods for these representations. Given the tutorial's main focus on word-level representation, this section provides partial coverage but also pointers for further reading.

7. Ethics and bias (10 minutes) In this section we will talk about the implicit bias in vector representations of meaning, with a focus on gender bias and word representations. We will also overview some of the recent techniques for debiasing word embeddings from gender stereotypes and biases.

4 Breadth

The tutorial is largely based on a recent book written by the instructors published by the Synthesis Lectures on Human Language Technologies of Morgan and Claypool, titled "Embeddings in Natural Language Processing: Theory and Advances in Vector Representations of Meaning" (Pilehvar and Camacho-Collados, 2020). This book covers all the various techniques on vectors representations of meaning in detail, while in this tutorial we provide an overview of the main ideas, without getting into details. .

5 Prerequisites for the attendees

No special advanced requirements are required for the attendees, but a certain familiarity with linear algebra, natural language processing and machine learning would be desirable.

6 Small reading list

In addition to the main reference book (Pilehvar and Camacho-Collados, 2020), in the following we present some references that may be helpful for understanding the tutorial. Nonetheless, they are not required to read in advance as their main ideas are also covered as part of the tutorial.

- Schütze (1992): Dimensions of meaning
- Turney and Pantel (2010): From Frequency to Meaning: Vector Space Models of Semantics
- Mikolov et al. (2013): Efficient Estimation of Word Representations in Vector Space
- Pennington et al. (2014): GloVe: Global vectors for word representation
- Melamud et al. (2016): Context2vec: Learning Generic Context Embedding with Bidirectional LSTM
- Peters et al. (2018a): Deep contextualized word representations
- Camacho-Collados and Pilehvar (2018): From word to sense embeddings: A survey on vector representations of meaning
- Peters et al. (2018b): Dissecting Contextual Word Embeddings: Architecture and Representation
- Devlin et al. (2018): BERT: Pre-training of Deep Bidirectional Transformers for Language Understanding

7 Instructors

Jose Camacho Collados (camachocolladosj@cardiff.ac.uk; `http://www.josecamachocollados.com`) is a UKRI Future Leaders Fellow and Lecturer at the School of Computer Science and Informatics at Cardiff University (United Kingdom). Previously he was a Google Doctoral Fellow, completed his PhD at Sapienza University of Rome (Italy) and had pre-doctoral experience as a statistical research engineer in France. His background education includes an Erasmus Mundus Masters in Human Language Technology and a 5-year BSc degree in Mathematics (Spain). Jose's main area of expertise is Natural Language Processing (NLP) and in particular computational semantics or, in other words, how to make computers understand language. His research has pivoted around both scientific contributions through regular publications in top AI and NLP venues such as ACL, EMNLP, AAAI or IJCAI; and applications with direct impact in society, with a special focus on social media and multilinguality. He has also organised several international workshops, tutorials and open challenges with hundreds of participants across the world.

Mohammad Taher Pilehvar (mp792@cam.ac.uk, `http://pilehvar.github.io`) is an Assistant Professor at Tehran Institute for Advanced Studies (TeIAS) and an Affiliated Lecturer at the University of Cambridge. Taher's research lies in lexical semantics, mainly focusing on semantic representation and similarity. In the past, he has co-instructed three tutorials on these topics (EMNLP 2015, ACL 2016, and EACL 2017) and co-organised three SemEval tasks and an EACL workshop on sense representations. He has also co-authored several conference papers (including two ACL best paper nominations, at 2013 and 2017).

References

Piotr Bojanowski, Edouard Grave, Armand Joulin, and Tomas Mikolov. 2017. Enriching word vectors with subword information. *Transactions of the Association of Computational Linguistics*, 5(1):135–146.

Jose Camacho-Collados and Mohammad Taher Pilehvar. 2018. From word to sense embeddings: A survey on vector representations of meaning. *Journal of Artificial Intelligence Research*, 63:743–788.

Jacob Devlin, Ming-Wei Chang, Kenton Lee, and Kristina Toutanova. 2018. BERT: pre-training of deep bidirectional transformers for language understanding. *CoRR*, abs/1810.04805.

William A. Gale, Kenneth Church, and David Yarowsky. 1992. A method for disambiguating word senses in a corpus. *Computers and the Humanities*, 26:415–439.

Eric H. Huang, Richard Socher, Christopher D. Manning, and Andrew Y. Ng. 2012. Improving word representations via global context and multiple word prototypes. In *Proceedings of ACL*, pages 873–882, Jeju Island, Korea.

Jiwei Li and Dan Jurafsky. 2015. Do multi-sense embeddings improve natural language understanding? In *Proceedings of EMNLP*, pages 683–693, Lisbon, Portugal.

Massimiliano Mancini, Jose Camacho-Collados, Ignacio Iacobacci, and Roberto Navigli. 2017. Embedding words and senses together via joint knowledge-enhanced training. In *Proceedings of CoNLL*, pages 100–111, Vancouver, Canada.

Oren Melamud, Jacob Goldberger, and Ido Dagan. 2016. context2vec: Learning generic context embedding with bidirectional lstm. In *Proceedings of The 20th SIGNLL Conference on Computational Natural Language Learning*, pages 51–61, Berlin, Germany.

Tomas Mikolov, Kai Chen, Greg Corrado, and Jeffrey Dean. 2013. Efficient estimation of word representations in vector space. *CoRR*, abs/1301.3781.

Arvind Neelakantan, Jeevan Shankar, Alexandre Passos, and Andrew McCallum. 2014. Efficient non-parametric estimation of multiple embeddings per word in vector space. In *Proceedings of EMNLP*, pages 1059–1069, Doha, Qatar.

Jeffrey Pennington, Richard Socher, and Christopher D Manning. 2014. GloVe: Global vectors for word representation. In *Proceedings of EMNLP*, pages 1532–1543.

Matthew Peters, M. Neumann, M. Iyyer, M. Gardner, C. Clark, K. Lee, and L. Zettlemoyer. 2018a. Deep contextualized word representations. In *Proceedings of NAACL*, New Orleans, LA, USA.

Matthew Peters, Mark Neumann, Luke Zettlemoyer, and Wen-tau Yih. 2018b. Dissecting contextual word embeddings: Architecture and representation. In *Proceedings of the 2018 Conference on Empirical Methods in Natural Language Processing*, pages 1499–1509, Brussels, Belgium, October-November. Association for Computational Linguistics.

Mohammad Taher Pilehvar and Jose Camacho-Collados. 2020. Embeddings in natural language processing: Theory and advances in vector representations of meaning. *Synthesis Lectures on Human Language Technologies*, 13(4):1–175.

Mohammad Taher Pilehvar and Nigel Collier. 2016. De-conflated semantic representations. In *Proceedings of EMNLP*, pages 1680–1690, Austin, TX.

Joseph Reisinger and Raymond J. Mooney. 2010. Multi-prototype vector-space models of word meaning. In *Proceedings of ACL*, pages 109–117.

Sascha Rothe and Hinrich Schütze. 2015. Autoextend: Extending word embeddings to embeddings for synsets and lexemes. In *Proceedings of ACL*, pages 1793–1803, Beijing, China.

Hinrich Schütze. 1992. Dimensions of meaning. In *Supercomputing '92: Proceedings of the 1992 ACM/IEEE conference on Supercomputing*, pages 787–796, Los Alamitos, CA, USA.

Peter D. Turney and Patrick Pantel. 2010. From frequency to meaning: Vector space models of semantics. *Journal of Artificial Intelligence Research*, 37:141–188.

Amos Tversky and Itamar Gati. 1982. Similarity, separability, and the triangle inequality. *Psychological Review*, 89(2):123.

Ashish Vaswani, Noam Shazeer, Niki Parmar, Jakob Uszkoreit, Llion Jones, Aidan N Gomez, Ł ukasz Kaiser, and Illia Polosukhin. 2017. Attention is all you need. In *Advances in Neural Information Processing Systems 30*, pages 5998–6008.

George K. Zipf. 1949. *Human Behaviour and the Principle of Least-Effort*. Addison-Wesley, Cambridge, MA.

Multilingual Neural Machine Translation

Raj Dabre[1]
NICT
Kyoto, Japan.

Chenhui Chu[2]
Kyoto University
Kyoto, Japan.

Anoop Kunchukuttan[3]
Microsoft
Hyderabad, India.

[1]raj.dabre@nict.go.jp, [2]chu@i.kyoto-u.ac.jp,
[3]anoop.kunchukuttan@microsoft.com

Abstract

The advent of neural machine translation (NMT) has opened up exciting research in building multilingual translation systems i.e. translation models that can handle more than one language pair. Many advances have been made which have enabled (1) improving translation for low-resource languages via transfer learning from high resource languages; and (2) building compact translation models spanning multiple languages. In this tutorial, we will cover the latest advances in NMT approaches that leverage multilingualism, especially to enhance low-resource translation. In particular, we will focus on the following topics: modeling parameter sharing for multi-way models, massively multilingual models, training protocols, language divergence, transfer learning, zero-shot/zero-resource learning, pivoting, multilingual pre-training and multi-source translation.

1 Relevance to CL community

Machine translation (MT) is one of the most challenging problems in CL and AI, and MT research has been at the forefront of many advances in the field. Since its advent in 2014, neural machine translation (NMT) (Sutskever et al., 2014; Bahdanau et al., 2015) has become the dominant paradigm and has shown the benefits of deep learning for NLP. While initial research on NMT started with building translation systems between two languages, researchers discovered that the NMT framework can naturally incorporate multiple languages. We refer to NMT systems handling translation between more than one language pair as *multilinugal NMT* (MNMT) systems.

There are multiple use cases and benefits for MNMT systems: (1) improving translation for low-resource languages via transfer learning from high-resource languages; (2) better generalization from exposure to diverse languages; (3) building compact translation models spanning multiple languages; (4) rapidly building MT systems by adapting existing multilingual models. In the past few years, there has been a lot of research addressing these themes and the area continues to be actively researched. Hence, it would be timely to have a tutorial which systematically presents the cutting-edge work in the area of MNMT. This would be of interest to researchers and practitioners of MT.

More broadly, multilingual NLP has received a lot of interest in recent times driven by two important questions:

Q1. *How do we build distributed representations such that similar text across languages have similar representations?*

Q2. *Is it possible to have a one-model-for-all-languages solution to NLP applications despite lacking data for certain languages?*

We believe that MNMT is a natural starting point to investigate these two important questions for NLP research. Hence, the tutorial would also be of interest to researchers and practitioners who work on multilingual NLP.

Proceedings of the 28th International Conference on Computational Linguistics: Tutorial Abstracts, pages 16–21
Barcelona, Spain (Online), December 12th, 2020.

2 Tutorial Overview

The tutorial will draw material from a survey paper on multilingual NMT that we have authored (Dabre et al., 2020). This paper has been published in ACM Computing Surveys. We also intend to cover some latest advances that are not mentioned in the survey paper. We will divide the tutorial in two parts, the first focusing on general purpose multilingual modeling and the second focusing on multiple usecases for multilingual NMT.

In the first part, we will first present an overview of the basics of NMT and cross-lingual embeddings. We will establish the fundamentals of MNMT and focus on various design choices. Design choices will involve network architecture, training protocols, data processing, hyper-parameter tuning so that they can successfully incorporate multilingualism. We will discuss specific changes to be made for translation between related languages as well as unrelated languages. We will also talk about the limits of massively MNMT models and provide a cost-benefit analysis from the perspective of deploying such models.

In the latter half of the tutorial, we will first focus on the challenging scenario of translation between language pairs for which there are few or no parallel corpora. We will introduce various ways to leverage pivot languages and on transfer learning approaches. We will show how transfer learning approaches such as fine-tuning and teacher-student learning can be optimally done when language relatedness and syntax are explicitly addressed. We will also touch upon unsupervised NMT which addresses low-resource MT using just monolingual corpora and is complimentary to NMT. We will see how multilingualism and unsupervised approaches can be combined. We will see how MT models for new languages can be rapidly adapted from pre-trained MNMT models. Additionally, we will spend some time on multi-source NMT which leverages multilingual redundancy in terms of input in order to yield high quality translations. We will end the tutorial with a discussion on possible future directions that we believe that MNMT research should take.

3 Tutorial Outline

Some representative papers are mentioned against tutorial sections.

1. Introduction (15 min)
   - Why MNMT?
   - Motivating multilingual NLP
   - Cross-lingual embeddings (Conneau et al., 2018; Jawanpuria et al., 2019)
   - Tutorial roadmap
2. Basics of NMT (20 min) (Sutskever et al., 2014; Bahdanau et al., 2015; Sennrich et al., 2016b; Sennrich et al., 2016a; Vaswani et al., 2017)
   - Architectures (RNN/Transformer)
   - Pre-processing and training
   - Decoding (beam-search, reranking)
3. Multi-way translation (45min) (Firat et al., 2016a; Johnson et al., 2017)
   - Prototypical architectures
   - Controlling parameter sharing (Sachan and Neubig, 2018; Platanios et al., 2018; Wang et al., 2018)
   - Addressing language divergence (Vázquez et al., 2018; Gu et al., 2018)
   - Training protocols (Tan et al., 2019; Lakew et al., 2018)
   - Massively multilingual models (Aharoni et al., 2019; Bapna et al., 2019)
4. – Coffee Break –

5. Transfer learning (30min)
   - Fine-tuning approaches (Zoph et al., 2016; Firat et al., 2016b)
   - Utilizing language relatedness (Dabre et al., 2017b; Kocmi and Bojar, 2018)
   - Lexical and syntactic transfer (Nguyen and Chiang, 2017; Murthy et al., 2019)
   - Rapid adaption of MT models (Neubig and Hu, 2018; Gheini and May, 2019)
6. Zero-shot/zero-resource learning (30 min) (Johnson et al., 2017; Firat et al., 2016b; Cheng et al., 2017)
   - Pivoting strategies
   - Modified training objectives (Al-Shedivat and Parikh, 2019)
   - Teacher-student learning (Chen et al., 2017)
   - Unsupervised learning (Lample et al., 2018; Xia et al., 2019; Sen et al., 2019)
7. Multi-source translation (15 min) (Zoph and Knight, 2016; Dabre et al., 2017a)
   - Missing sentences (Nishimura et al., 2018)
   - Hybrid multi-source systems
   - Post-editing (Chatterjee et al., 2017)
8. Future directions (15 min)
9. Summary and conclusion (10 min)

Total Time: 180 minutes (excluding break).
Type of the Tutorial: Cutting-edge.
Pre-requisites: Familiarity with sequence to sequence learning.

4 Tutorial Instructors

Dr. Raj Dabre

Post-Doctoral Researcher, NICT, Kyoto, Japan
email: raj.dabre@nict.go.jp
website: https://prajdabre.wixsite.com/prajdabre

Raj Dabre received his M.Tech. from IIT Bombay, India and his Ph.D. from Kyoto University, Japan. He is a post-doctoral researcher at NICT which is Japan's national research institution for communication technologies. His research interests center on natural language processing, particularly neural machine translation for low resource languages and on model compression and computing efficiency. He has MT-related publications in ACL, EMNLP, AAAI, NAACL, COLING, INTERSPEECH and WMT. He was a member of the organizing committee of COLING 2012, is a current member of the organizing committee of the Workshop on Asian Translation and has coordinated joint research between Kyoto University (Japan) and IIT Bombay (India).

Dr. Chenhui Chu

Program-Specific Associate Professor, Graduate School Of Informatics, Kyoto University, Japan.
email: chu@i.kyoto-u.ac.jp
website: http://researchmap.jp/chu/?lang=english

Chenhui Chu received his B.S. in Software Engineering from Chongqing University in 2008, and M.S., and Ph.D. in Informatics from Kyoto University in 2012 and 2015, respectively. He is currently a program-specific associate professor at Kyoto University. His research won the MSRA collaborative research 2019 grant award, 2018 AAMT Nagao award, and CICLing 2014 best student paper award. He is on the editorial board of the Journal of Natural Language Processing, Journal of Information

Processing, and a steering committee member of Young Researcher Association for NLP Studies. His research interests center on natural language processing, particularly machine translation and language and vision understanding.

Dr. Anoop Kunchukuttan

Senior Applied Researcher, Microsoft, Hyderabad, India.
email: anoop.kunchukuttan@microsoft.com
website: http://anoopk.in
Anoop Kunchukuttan is a Senior Applied Researcher in the MT team at Microsoft India, where he is involved in building MT systems for multiple Indian languages. His research interests span in different aspects of machine translation, particularly: multilingual models, low-resource translation and translation involving related languages. More broadly, he is interested in different multilingual, cross-lingual and multi-task NLP approaches. He is passionate about building software and resources for NLP in Indian languages. He is the developer of the *Indic NLP Library* (Kunchukuttan, 2020), co-developer of the IndicNLP-Suite (Kakwani et al., 2020) and a co-founder of the AI4Bharat-NLP Initiative, a community initiative to build Indian language NLP technologies. He has published papers on MT and multilingual learning at ACL, NAACL, EMNLP, TACL and IJCNLP. He has been a member of the organizing committees for COLING 2012 and Workshop on Asian Translation. He received his Ph.D from the Indian Institute of Technology Bombay.

References

Roee Aharoni, Melvin Johnson, and Orhan Firat. 2019. Massively Multilingual Neural Machine Translation. In *NAACL*.

Maruan Al-Shedivat and Ankur Parikh. 2019. Consistency by agreement in zero-shot neural machine translation. In *NAACL*.

Dzmitry Bahdanau, Kyunghyun Cho, and Yoshua Bengio. 2015. Neural machine translation by jointly learning to align and translate. In *In Proceedings of the 3rd International Conference on Learning Representations (ICLR 2015)*, San Diego, USA, May. International Conference on Learning Representations.

Ankur Bapna, Colin Andrew Cherry, Dmitry (Dima) Lepikhin, George Foster, Maxim Krikun, Melvin Johnson, Mia Chen, Naveen Ari, Orhan Firat, Wolfgang Macherey, Yonghui Wu, Yuan Cao, and Zhifeng Chen. 2019. Massively multilingual neural machine translation in the wild: Findings and challenges. *arXiv:1907.05019*.

Rajen Chatterjee, M. Amin Farajian, Matteo Negri, Marco Turchi, Ankit Srivastava, and Santanu Pal. 2017. Multi-source neural automatic post-editing: Fbk's participation in the WMT 2017 ape shared task. In *Proceedings of the Second Conference on Machine Translation*, pages 630–638. Association for Computational Linguistics.

Yun Chen, Yang Liu, Yong Cheng, and Victor O.K. Li. 2017. A teacher-student framework for zero-resource neural machine translation. In *Proceedings of the 55th Annual Meeting of the Association for Computational Linguistics (Volume 1: Long Papers)*, pages 1925–1935. Association for Computational Linguistics.

Yong Cheng, Qian Yang, Yang Liu, Maosong Sun, and Wei Xu. 2017. Joint training for pivot-based neural machine translation. In *Proceedings of the Twenty-Sixth International Joint Conference on Artificial Intelligence, IJCAI-17*, pages 3974–3980.

Alexis Conneau, Guillaume Lample, Marc'Aurelio Ranzato, Ludovic Denoyer, and Hervé Jégou. 2018. Word translation without parallel data. In *Proceedings of the International Conference on Learning Representations*. URL: `https://github.com/facebookresearch/MUSE`.

Raj Dabre, Fabien Cromieres, and Sadao Kurohashi. 2017a. Enabling multi-source neural machine translation by concatenating source sentences in multiple languages. In *Proceedings of MT Summit XVI, vol.1: Research Track*, pages 96–106.

Raj Dabre, Tetsuji Nakagawa, and Hideto Kazawa. 2017b. An empirical study of language relatedness for transfer learning in neural machine translation. In *Proceedings of the 31st Pacific Asia Conference on Language, Information and Computation*, pages 282–286. The National University (Phillippines).

Raj Dabre, Chenhui Chu, and Anoop Kunchukuttan. 2020. A Survey of Multilingual Neural Machine Translation. *ACM Computing Surveys*, 53(5), September.

Orhan Firat, Kyunghyun Cho, and Yoshua Bengio. 2016a. Multi-way, multilingual neural machine translation with a shared attention mechanism. In *Proceedings of the 2016 Conference of the North American Chapter of the Association for Computational Linguistics: Human Language Technologies*, pages 866–875. Association for Computational Linguistics.

Orhan Firat, Baskaran Sankaran, Yaser Al-Onaizan, Fatos T. Yarman Vural, and Kyunghyun Cho. 2016b. Zero-resource translation with multi-lingual neural machine translation. In *Proceedings of the 2016 Conference on Empirical Methods in Natural Language Processing*, pages 268–277. Association for Computational Linguistics.

Mozhdeh Gheini and Jonathan May. 2019. A universal parent model for low-resource neural machine translation transfer. *arXiv:1909.06516*.

Jiatao Gu, Hany Hassan, Jacob Devlin, and Victor O.K. Li. 2018. Universal neural machine translation for extremely low resource languages. In *Proceedings of the 2018 Conference of the North American Chapter of the Association for Computational Linguistics: Human Language Technologies, Volume 1 (Long Papers)*, pages 344–354. Association for Computational Linguistics.

Pratik Jawanpuria, Arjun Balgovind, Anoop Kunchukuttan, and Bamdev Mishra. 2019. Learning multilingual word embeddings in latent metric space: a geometric approach. *Transaction of the Association for Computational Linguistics (TACL).*

Melvin Johnson, Mike Schuster, Quoc V. Le, Maxim Krikun, Yonghui Wu, Zhifeng Chen, Nikhil Thorat, Fernanda Viégas, Martin Wattenberg, Greg Corrado, Macduff Hughes, and Jeffrey Dean. 2017. Google's multilingual neural machine translation system: Enabling zero-shot translation. *Transactions of the Association for Computational Linguistics*, 5:339–351.

Divyanshu Kakwani, Anoop Kunchukuttan, Satish Golla, Gokul N.C., Avik Bhattacharyya, Mitesh M. Khapra, and Pratyush Kumar. 2020. IndicNLPSuite: Monolingual corpora, evaluation benchmarks and pre-trained multilingual language models for Indian languages. In *Findings of the Association for Computational Linguistics: EMNLP 2020*, pages 4948–4961, Online, November. Association for Computational Linguistics.

Tom Kocmi and OndÅ™ej Bojar. 2018. Trivial transfer learning for low-resource neural machine translation. In *Proceedings of the Third Conference on Machine Translation, Volume 1: Research Papers*, pages 244–252, Belgium, Brussels, October. Association for Computational Linguistics.

Anoop Kunchukuttan. 2020. The IndicNLP Library. `https://github.com/anoopkunchukuttan/indic_nlp_library/blob/master/docs/indicnlp.pdf`.

Surafel Melaku Lakew, Aliia Erofeeva, Matteo Negri, Marcello Federico, and Marco Turchi. 2018. Transfer learning in multilingual neural machine translation with dynamic vocabulary. In *IWSLT*.

Guillaume Lample, Alexis Conneau, Ludovic Denoyer, and Marc'Aurelio Ranzato. 2018. Unsupervised machine translation using monolingual corpora only. In *International Conference on Learning Representations*.

V. Rudra Murthy, Anoop Kunchukuttan, and Pushpak Bhattacharyya. 2019. Addressing word-order divergence in multilingual neural machine translation for extremely low resource languages. In *NAACL*.

Graham Neubig and Junjie Hu. 2018. Rapid adaptation of neural machine translation to new languages. In *Proceedings of the 2018 Conference on Empirical Methods in Natural Language Processing*, pages 875–880. Association for Computational Linguistics.

Toan Q. Nguyen and David Chiang. 2017. Transfer learning across low-resource, related languages for neural machine translation. In *Proceedings of the Eighth International Joint Conference on Natural Language Processing (Volume 2: Short Papers)*, pages 296–301. Asian Federation of Natural Language Processing.

Yuta Nishimura, Katsuhito Sudoh, Graham Neubig, and Satoshi Nakamura. 2018. Multi-source neural machine translation with data augmentation. In *15th International Workshop on Spoken Language Translation (IWSLT)*, Brussels, Belgium, October.

Emmanouil Antonios Platanios, Mrinmaya Sachan, Graham Neubig, and Tom Mitchell. 2018. Contextual parameter generation for universal neural machine translation. In *Proceedings of the 2018 Conference on Empirical Methods in Natural Language Processing*, pages 425–435. Association for Computational Linguistics.

Devendra Sachan and Graham Neubig. 2018. Parameter sharing methods for multilingual self-attentional translation models. In *Proceedings of the Third Conference on Machine Translation: Research Papers*, pages 261–271. Association for Computational Linguistics.

Sukanta Sen, Kamal Kumar Gupta, Asif Ekbal, and Pushpak Bhattacharyya. 2019. Multilingual unsupervised nmt using shared encoder and language-specific decoders. In *Proceedings of the 57th Annual Meeting of the Association for Computational Linguistics.*

Rico Sennrich, Barry Haddow, and Alexandra Birch. 2016a. Improving neural machine translation models with monolingual data. In *Proceedings of the 54th Annual Meeting of the Association for Computational Linguistics (Volume 1: Long Papers)*, pages 86–96, Berlin, Germany, August. Association for Computational Linguistics.

Rico Sennrich, Barry Haddow, and Alexandra Birch. 2016b. Neural machine translation of rare words with subword units. In *Proceedings of the 54th Annual Meeting of the Association for Computational Linguistics (Volume 1: Long Papers)*, pages 1715–1725, Berlin, Germany, August. Association for Computational Linguistics.

Ilya Sutskever, Oriol Vinyals, and Quoc V. Le. 2014. Sequence to sequence learning with neural networks. In *Proceedings of the 27th International Conference on Neural Information Processing Systems*, NIPS'14, pages 3104–3112, Cambridge, MA, USA. MIT Press.

Xu Tan, Yi Ren, Di He, Tao Qin, and Tie-Yan Liu. 2019. Multilingual neural machine translation with knowledge distillation. In *International Conference on Learning Representations.*

Ashish Vaswani, Noam Shazeer, Niki Parmar, Jakob Uszkoreit, Llion Jones, Aidan N Gomez, Ł ukasz Kaiser, and Illia Polosukhin. 2017. Attention is all you need. In I. Guyon, U. V. Luxburg, S. Bengio, H. Wallach, R. Fergus, S. Vishwanathan, and R. Garnett, editors, *Advances in Neural Information Processing Systems 30*, pages 5998–6008. Curran Associates, Inc.

Raúl Vázquez, Alessandro Raganato, Jörg Tiedemann, and Mathias Creutz. 2018. Multilingual NMT with a language-independent attention bridge. *CoRR*, abs/1811.00498.

Yining Wang, Jiajun Zhang, Feifei Zhai, Jingfang Xu, and Chengqing Zong. 2018. Three strategies to improve one-to-many multilingual translation. In *Proceedings of the 2018 Conference on Empirical Methods in Natural Language Processing*, pages 2955–2960. Association for Computational Linguistics.

Mengzhou Xia, Xiang Kong, Antonios Anastasopoulos, and Graham Neubig. 2019. Generalized data augmentation for low-resource translation. In *ACL.*

Barret Zoph and Kevin Knight. 2016. Multi-source neural translation. In *Proceedings of the 2016 Conference of the North American Chapter of the Association for Computational Linguistics: Human Language Technologies*, pages 30–34. Association for Computational Linguistics.

Barret Zoph, Deniz Yuret, Jonathan May, and Kevin Knight. 2016. Transfer learning for low-resource neural machine translation. In *Proceedings of the 2016 Conference on Empirical Methods in Natural Language Processing, EMNLP 2016, Austin, Texas, USA, November 1-4, 2016*, pages 1568–1575.

Detection and Resolution of Rumors and Misinformation with NLP

Leon Derczynski
ITU Copenhagen, Denmark
ld@itu.dk

Arkaitz Zubiaga
Queen Mary University of London, UK
a.zubiaga@qmul.ac.uk

Abstract

Detecting and grounding false and misleading claims on the web has grown to form a substantial sub-field of NLP. The field addresses problems at multiple different levels of misinformation detection: identifying check-worthy claims; tracking claims and rumors; rumor collection and annotation; grounding claims against knowledge bases; using stance to verify claims; and applying style analysis to detect deception. This half-day tutorial presents the theory behind each of these steps as well as the state-of-the-art solutions.

1 Description

Now we know that information can be controlled by anyone, and that it can travel more quickly – from walking to another person and talking to them to tell a story, to the modern reality of clicking to share, or commenting in a discourse making it pop up on others' feeds – what is the impact? For misinformation, it is that claims move faster through the web than can be humanly fact-checked (Hassan et al., 2015; Starbird et al., 2014). This means that addressing the challenge of misinformation at scale requires technological solutions. This tutorial is broken down into the following sections:

1.1 Identifying check-worthy claims

Having a particular textual source as input, such as a TV debate, a social media stream or news articles, the claim detection task consists in identifying the sentences or segments that constitute claims that need verification or fact-checking (Konstantinovskiy et al., 2018). It can be defined as a binary classification task, where input sentences are classified as claims or non-claims, or alternatively as a ranking or regression task, where sentences are given a checkworthiness score.

1.2 Tracking claims and rumors

Having identified a checkworthy story, the next step is being able to track the story on the web as it spreads between outlets and social media platforms. To do this, we cover techniques from LSH (Petrović et al., 2010) to state-of-the-art techniques: the explicit detection of emerging claims (Popat et al., 2017) and use of RNN attention to follow a story as it develops (Chen et al., 2018).

1.3 Rumor collection and annotation

Collection of a dataset of rumors and its subsequent annotation is a challenging task as there are limitations of resources constraining how much one can afford to annotate, whereas one wants to collect a dataset as large as possible to make it representative and diverse. Different collection and sampling methods have been proposed for rumor data collection, including (i) methods that identify rumors a priori, manually defining a set of keywords that enable collection of relevant posts, and (ii) methods that identify rumors a posteriori, first collecting a large dataset of posts, e.g. starting off with the collection of posts associated with a particular event or collecting entire timelines of users, to then sample the data to a manageable size, e.g. by random sampling or popularity-based sampling (Zubiaga et al., 2015).

Proceedings of the 28th International Conference on Computational Linguistics: Tutorial Abstracts, pages 22–26
Barcelona, Spain (Online), December 12th, 2020.

1.4 Grounding claims against knowledge bases

Having found a claim on the web, the next step is to determine its veracity – to test if it is true or not. Depending on what the claim involves, and the context of the claim, there are a variety of techniques available. This section discusses those techniques, analyzing the claim itself and comparing with external factors – like the stance others take to the claim, or information stored in external knowledge bases.

An assessment of veracity is stronger if accompanied by supporting evidence. This is the approach taken in the FEVER challenge (Thorne et al., 2018), where supporting text must be provided alongside a judgment. We introduce techniques including word and entity matching between claim and article (Yoneda et al., 2018; Luken et al., 2018), neural whole-sentence comparison using Enhanced LSTM (Chen et al., 2016) or Decomposable Attention (Parikh et al., 2016), and the pros and cons of NLI-based techniques for rumour verification (Bowman et al., 2015; Rocktäschel et al., 2016).

1.5 Using stance to verify claims

It's not always possible to ground a claim to an authoritative source. Emerging claims may not yet be mentioned in resources like WikiData, due to lag; and claims around entities that are not notable enough for inclusion in knowledge bases will remain difficult to ground. However, the stance that social media users take to claims can serve to predict the claim's accuracy (Dungs et al., 2018; Qazvinian et al., 2011). In this part, we introduce the problem of stance prediction, discuss multiple framings of the problem, and describe the state-of-the-art in stance prediction with both neural and non-neural techniques (Augenstein et al., 2016; Aker et al., 2017). We go on to describe how stance predictions can be combined through multi-spaced HMM to predict veracity based on conversational stances (Dungs et al., 2018), and how models for this can be transferred across languages (Lillie et al., 2019).

1.6 Style analysis for deception detection

Many verification practices concentrate on determining precisely what the claim is, and then finding whether or not that claim is false. This misses an important and much closer source: the way in which the claim itself is written. Style tells us a lot about an author and their intent, and more candid the writing is, the more information an author leaks about themself. When people seek to deceive, they adopt a certain set of behaviors. These behaviors can affect how they use language, thus providing a stylistic clue to identifying deception and deceptive intent. This section of the tutorial introduces these techniques, explaining typical linguistic cues and outlining how they can be mined automatically (Zhou et al., 2004; Feng et al., 2012; Fitzpatrick et al., 2015), as well as introducing caveats for applying this technology in the context of fact checking.

2 Type

This is a "cutting edge" tutorial; none on the topic have been presented before at the relevant venues.

3 Structure outline

Introduction A contextualisation of the course material, including a brief history of fact checking and a challenging quiz around modern claims, at each step delineating the scope of what NLP-based methods can do to address each kind of misinformation.

Identifying and tracking check-worthy claims Define checkworthiness and modern techniques for automatically detecting it. Introduce classical and cutting-edge techniques for claim tracking.

Rumor collection and annotation We'll attempt to do some live collection here, of data in the participant's own language, to be used later

Grounding claims against knowledgebases 1 Introduce techniques, and introduce a practical exercise

Coffee break

Grounding claims against knowledgebases 2 Finish introducing techniques and apply one

Using stance to verify claims Introduce stance prediction and using stance to predict veracity; a brief annotation and prediction exercise using an existing cross-lingual model.

Style analysis for deception detection Introduce techniques for deception detection, based on writing style and also metadata; discuss when these are and are not applicable to data, and how to be careful to adapt to linguistic variation.

Summary & feedback How was it?

End Total: 3.5 hours.

4 Breadth

About 25% of the material in the tutorial covers the presenters' own work; the majority is by others. The subfield is quite broad, and so even by selecting a good subset of important and recent papers to present in the time given, it would be unusual for a single researcher's work to have spanned the subfield's entire gamut. See e.g. the breadth in the bibliography for this proposal.

5 Diversity considerations

We'll discuss techniques for multiple languages during the tutorial, and we hope to generate even more multilingual data through brief exercises in the tutorial. The presenters are affiliated in different countries (Denmark and UK) with different L1 (English and Basque). The tutorial includes some techniques that scale up to multiple languages (e.g. veracity prediction from stance). While both presenters are male, the senior primary investigators that got us into this and continue to lead in the field are both female (Kalina Bontcheva and Maria Liakata), so the tutorial comes from a background of gender diversity.

6 Prerequisites for attendees

Attendees should be reasonably fluent in Python and comfortable using notebooks; we'll try a few live exercises. Familiarity with the Twitter API is a bonus, and one should have an account before starting the exercises (we don't need to know what the account is, it's simply for getting a developer API key).

7 Presenters

One UK, one Denmark (two male).

Leon Derczynski is an assistant professor of Computer Science at the IT University of Copenhagen, Denmark. He was program co-chair for COLING 2018, co-author of an EU project on misinformation (Derczynski et al., 2015), PHEME, co-investigator of an EC Horizon 2020 RIA, Comrades, and has co-organised SemEval shared tasks in 2013/15/16/17/19 (e.g. (Gorrell et al., 2019)). He has published repeatedly in the area of rumour identification and processing and given talks on the topics at a wide range of venues, and teaches a course on NLP-based verification and misinformation detection at Innopolis University, Russia. Leon has taught full university courses in the UK, USA, Denmark, Russia, and China. `ld@itu.dk` `www.derczynski.com`.

Arkaitz Zubiaga is an assistant professor at Queen Mary University of London, UK. He is on the editorial boards of the Information Processing & Management, Online Social Networks and Media, PeerJ Computer Science, and Information journals. He has published extensively on misinformation both within and beyond NLP venues, and has co-organised multiple SemEval and other evaluation tasks and workshops around misinformation. `a.zubiaga@qmul.ac.uk` `https://www.zubiaga.org`.

8 Audience size estimate

A social media processing tutorial at EACL 2014 attracted circa 30 audience members. With our field's overall growth, the global nature of the host conference, and the popularity of the subject, we expect an audience of 50-150 depending on venue.

9 Equipment requirements

Standard AV setup; decent internet required, so it might be beneficial if the tutorial was not held on a main conference day or on the same day as a major workshop (e.g. WMT).

10 Open access

We agree to allow the publication of your slides and video recording of your tutorial in the ACL Anthology. Our teaching material will be made openly available from the day of the tutorial.

References

Ahmet Aker, Leon Derczynski, and Kalina Bontcheva. 2017. Simple open stance classification for rumour analysis. In *Proceedings of the International Conference Recent Advances in Natural Language Processing.*

Isabelle Augenstein, Tim Rocktäschel, Andreas Vlachos, and Kalina Bontcheva. 2016. Stance Detection with Bidirectional Conditional Encoding. In *Proceedings of the 2016 Conference on Empirical Methods in Natural Language Processing*, pages 876–885.

Samuel R Bowman, Gabor Angeli, Christopher Potts, and Christopher D Manning. 2015. A large annotated corpus for learning natural language inference. In *Proceedings of the Conference on Empirical Methods in Natural Language Processing*, pages 632–642.

Qian Chen, Xiaodan Zhu, Zhenhua Ling, Si Wei, Hui Jiang, and Diana Inkpen. 2016. Enhanced LSTM for natural language inference. In *Proceedings of ACL.*

Tong Chen, Xue Li, Hongzhi Yin, and Jun Zhang. 2018. Call attention to rumors: Deep attention based recurrent neural networks for early rumor detection. In *Pacific-Asia Conference on Knowledge Discovery and Data Mining*, pages 40–52. Springer.

Leon Derczynski, Kalina Bontcheva, Michal Lukasik, Thierry Declerck, Arno Scharl, Georgi Georgiev, Petya Osenova, Toms Pariente Lobo, Anna Kolliakou, Robert Stewart, Sara-Jayne Terp, Geraldine Wong, Christian Burger, Arkaitz Zubiaga, Rob Procter, and Maria Liakata. 2015. PHEME: Computing Veracity – the Fourth Challenge of Big Social Data. In *Proceedings of the Extended Semantic Web Conference EU Project Networking session (ESCW-PN).*

Sebastian Dungs, Ahmet Aker, Norbert Fuhr, and Kalina Bontcheva. 2018. Can rumour stance alone predict veracity? In *Proceedings of COLING*, pages 3360–3370.

Song Feng, Ritwik Banerjee, and Yejin Choi. 2012. Syntactic stylometry for deception detection. In *Proceedings of the 50th Annual Meeting of the Association for Computational Linguistics*, volume 2, pages 171–175. Association for Computational Linguistics.

Eileen Fitzpatrick, Joan Bachenko, and Tommaso Fornaciari. 2015. Automatic detection of verbal deception. *Synthesis Lectures on Human Language Technologies*, 8(3):1–119.

Genevieve Gorrell, Elena Kochkina, Maria Liakata, Ahmet Aker, Arkaitz Zubiaga, Kalina Bontcheva, and Leon Derczynski. 2019. SemEval-2019 task 7: RumourEval, determining rumour veracity and support for rumours. In *Proceedings of the 13th International Workshop on Semantic Evaluation*, pages 845–854, Minneapolis, Minnesota, USA, June. Association for Computational Linguistics.

Naeemul Hassan, Bill Adair, James Hamilton, Chengkai Li, Mark Tremayne, Jun Yang, and Cong Yu. 2015. The quest to automate fact-checking. In *Proceedings of the 2015 Computation+Journalism Symposium.*

Lev Konstantinovskiy, Oliver Price, Mevan Babakar, and Arkaitz Zubiaga. 2018. Towards Automated Factchecking: Developing an Annotation Schema and Benchmark for Consistent Automated Claim Detection. *arXiv preprint arXiv:1809.08193.*

Anders E Lillie, Emil Refsgaard Middelboe, and Leon Derczynski. 2019. Joint rumour stance and veracity. In *Proceedings of the Nordic Conference on Computational Linguistics (NODALIDA).* NEALT.

Jackson Luken, Nanjiang Jiang, and Marie-Catherine de Marneffe. 2018. QED: A fact verification system for the FEVER shared task. In *Proceedings of the First Workshop on Fact Extraction and VERification (FEVER)*, pages 156–160. Association for Computational Linguistics.

Ankur P Parikh, Oscar Täckström, Dipanjan Das, and Jakob Uszkoreit. 2016. A decomposable attention model for natural language inference. In *Proceedings of EMNLP*.

Saša Petrović, Miles Osborne, and Victor Lavrenko. 2010. Streaming first story detection with application to Twitter. In *Proceedings of the Annual Conference Of The North American Chapter Of The Association For Computational Linguistics*, pages 181–189. Association for Computational Linguistics.

Kashyap Popat, Subhabrata Mukherjee, Jannik Strötgen, and Gerhard Weikum. 2017. Where the truth lies: Explaining the credibility of emerging claims on the web and social media. In *Proceedings of the 26th International Conference on World Wide Web Companion*, pages 1003–1012. International World Wide Web Conferences Steering Committee.

Vahed Qazvinian, Emily Rosengren, Dragomir R Radev, and Qiaozhu Mei. 2011. Rumor has it: Identifying misinformation in microblogs. In *Proceedings of the Conference on Empirical Methods in Natural Language Processing*, pages 1589–1599. Association for Computational Linguistics.

Tim Rocktäschel, Edward Grefenstette, Karl Moritz Hermann, Tomáš Kočiský, and Phil Blunsom. 2016. Reasoning about entailment with neural attention. In *Proceedings of ICLR*.

Kate Starbird, Jim Maddock, Mania Orand, Peg Achterman, and Robert M Mason. 2014. Rumors, False Flags, and Digital Vigilantes: Misinformation on Twitter after the 2013 Boston marathon bombing. *Proceedings of the iConference*.

James Thorne, Andreas Vlachos, Christos Christodoulopoulos, and Arpit Mittal. 2018. FEVER: a large-scale dataset for Fact Extraction and VERification. In *Proceedings of NAACL*.

Takuma Yoneda, Jeff Mitchell, Johannes Welbl, Pontus Stenetorp, and Sebastian Riedel. 2018. UCL Machine Reading Group: Four Factor Framework For Fact Finding (HexaF). In *Proceedings of the First Workshop on Fact Extraction and VERification (FEVER)*, pages 97–102. Association for Computational Linguistics.

Lina Zhou, Judee K Burgoon, Jay F Nunamaker, and Doug Twitchell. 2004. Automating linguistics-based cues for detecting deception in text-based asynchronous computer-mediated communications. *Group decision and negotiation*, 13(1):81–106.

Arkaitz Zubiaga, Maria Liakata, Rob Procter, Kalina Bontcheva, and Peter Tolmie. 2015. Crowdsourcing the annotation of rumourous conversations in social media. In *Proceedings of the 24th International Conference on World Wide Web*, pages 347–353. ACM.

A guide to the dataset explosion in QA, NLI, and commonsense reasoning

Anna Rogers
Center for Social Data Science
University of Copenhagen
Copenhagen, Denmark
arogers@sodas.ku.dk

Anna Rumshisky
Dept. of Computer Science
Univ. of Massachusetts Lowell
Lowell, USA
arum@cs.uml.edu

Abstract

Question answering, natural language inference and commonsense reasoning are increasingly popular as general NLP system benchmarks, driving both modeling and dataset work. Only for question answering we already have over 100 datasets, with over 40 published after 2018. However, most new datasets get "solved" soon after publication, and this is largely due not to the verbal reasoning capabilities of our models, but to annotation artifacts and shallow cues in the data that they can exploit.

This tutorial aims to (1) provide an up-to-date guide to the recent datasets, (2) survey the old and new methodological issues with dataset construction, and (3) outline the existing proposals for overcoming them. The target audience is the NLP practitioners who are lost in dozens of the recent datasets, and would like to know what these datasets are actually measuring. Our overview of the problems with the current datasets and the latest tips and tricks in the dataset construction methodology will also be useful to the researchers working on future benchmarks. The tutorial slides are available online at https://www.annargrs.github.io/dataset-explosion.

1 Tutorial description

High-level verbal reasoning tasks are increasingly used as de-facto Turing test proxies in evaluating the language capabilities of NLP systems. In particular, question answering (QA), natural language inference (NLI) and commonsense reasoning are included in evaluation suites and featured in most papers proposing new architectures. Accordingly, these tasks are seeing an explosion of datasets: there are already over 100 datasets only for QA, with over 40 published since 2018. This makes the choice of data for a given study a research-intensive task in itself.

The goals of the tutorial are as follows:

- to provide an up-to-date guide to the recent datasets for training verbal reasoning systems;
- to survey the old and new methodological issues;
- to outline the existing proposals for overcoming them, and to highlight the biggest remaining challenges.

This tutorial would be useful to NLP practitioners who simply want to pick a dataset and focus on modeling work, while being aware of potential issues that often go unnoticed. It would also be useful to the researchers working on new datasets and looking for the latest tips and tricks for overcoming the common pitfalls.

2 Details and Prerequisites

The tutorial will be of the *cutting-edge* type. The tutorial slides are available online at https://www.annargrs.github.io/dataset-explosion.

Prerequisites. We assume basic familiarity with the standard machine learning evaluation workflow and the three tasks that we are covering (question answering, commonsense reasoning, natural language inference). We also assume some familiarity with the methodology of crowdsourcing NLP datasets.

Proceedings of the 28th International Conference on Computational Linguistics: Tutorial Abstracts, pages 27–32
Barcelona, Spain (Online), December 12th, 2020.

3 Reading list

The core approaches to machine reading comprehension and several widely-used datasets are covered in the survey by Qui et al. (2019). For NLI, we refer the reader to the surveys on resources and approaches (Storks et al., 2019b), as well as issues with the current data (Schlegel et al., 2020). A survey on benchmarks and approaches is also available for commonsense reasoning (Storks et al., 2019a).

4 Tutorial outline

The tutorial will present three hours of content with a thirty minute break.

Motivation. We will start by discussing the place of high-level reasoning tasks in the current NLP system evaluation paradigm: how the focus shifted away from the the low-level tasks such as POS-tagging, and how the low-level linguistic competences seems to be coming back (Ribeiro et al., 2020).

The dataset explosion. This first part of the tutorial will provide an overview of the main types of datasets for QA, NLI, and commonsense reasoning. For each sub-type, we will discuss representative dataset examples.

The field of question answering encompasses both open-world QA and reading comprehension (RC). Open-world QA focuses on factoid questions, with the answers typically extracted from web snippets or Wikipedia. The questions usually come from search engine queries (Kwiatkowski et al., 2019) and quiz data (Joshi et al., 2017). Bordering on open-world QA is the task of QA on structured data, such as tables and databases (Jiang et al., 2019).

Most current reading comprehension datasets are extractive (Rajpurkar et al., 2016; Dua et al., 2019), i.e. the correct answer is contained within the text itself, and the task is to find the correct span. Multiple-choice questions are harder to generate, as they need good confounds, and often come from curated test collections (Lai et al., 2017). Freeform answers remain rare (Bajaj et al., 2016), as evaluating them faces the general problem of evaluating language generation. Most RC datasets are single-domain, with a few exceptions (Reddy et al., 2018).

For NLI, we will organize the discussion in terms of domains covered by the current datasets: single-domain (Bowman et al., 2015), multi-domain (Williams et al., 2017), specialized domains (Romanov and Shivade, 2018). In both QA and NLI there have also been attempts to recast datasets from other tasks as QA/NLI problems (McCann et al., 2018; White et al., 2017), and researchers working on NLI often rely on the datasets for the related problem of RTE (Dzikovska et al., 2013).

Commonsense reasoning datasets come in different formats: multi-choice reading comprehension (Ostermann et al., 2018), extractive reading comprehension (Zhang et al., 2018), story completion (Mostafazadeh et al., 2017) and also as multi-choice questions for a single sentence input (Levesque et al., 2012). The task of commonsense reasoning is supposed to involve a combination of context-internal knowledge with context-external world knowledge, and we will briefly mention the major sources of such knowledge that are typically recommended in commonsense challenges, such as scripts (Wanzare et al., 2016), frames (Baker et al., 1998), and entity relations (Speer et al., 2017).

Reality check. One of the reasons there are so many new datasets is that most of them get "solved" very soon after publication, as it happened with CoQA (Reddy et al., 2018). However, this is not necessarily a testimony to the linguistic power of deep learning. It is becoming increasingly clear that, given the opportunity, our models exploit annotation artifacts and shallow lexical cues, achieving a high performance but not a high degree of language understanding. The second part of the tutorial will synthesize a string of papers exposing such issues (Niven and Kao, 2019; McCoy et al., 2019; Geva et al., 2019; Wallace et al., 2019).

To give a few examples, for QA it has been shown that human-level performance on SQuADcan be achieved while relying only on superficial cues (Jia and Liang, 2017), and 73% of the NewsQA can be solved by simply identifying the single most relevant sentence (Chen et al., 2016). A system trained on one QA dataset does not tend to perform well on another one, even if it is in the same domain (Yatskar, 2019). Research on adversarial attacks suggests that it is possible to find dataset-specific phrases that will force a QA system to output a certain prediction when added to any input. For example, a SQuAD-trained QA system can be hacked in this way to always predict "to kill Americam people" as the answer to any question (Wallace et al., 2019).

In NLI, 67% of SNLI (Bowman et al., 2015) and 53% of MultiNLI (Williams et al., 2017) can be solved without looking at the premise (Gururangan et al., 2018). The HANS dataset showed that models trained on MNLI (Williams et al., 2017) actually learn to rely on shallow cues and can be fooled by syntactic heuristics (McCoy et al., 2019). Furthermore, the models trained on such datasets are unaware of lexical knowledge that would have enabled them to solve simple WordNet-based permutations of the original data (Glockner et al., 2018).

In commonsense reasoning, by definition, the challenge is to get the system to make decision based on both the current context and some general knowledge about the world. However, in the challenge of SemEval2018-Task 11 (Ostermann et al., 2018) most participants did not use any extra knowledge sources, and one of them still achieved 0.82 accuracy vs 0.84 achieved by the ConceptNet-based winner. It is argued that large pre-trained language models already possess much of such knowledge: for instance, BERT (Devlin et al., 2018) achieved over 86% on SWAG (Zellers et al., 2018).

We will also mention the widespread methodological problem of under-reporting of environment factors that may make as much difference as the proposed architecture changes. The effect of such factors as random seed, hardware, library versions has been discussed for several QA datasets (Crane, 2018).

Methodology developments and challenges. For existing datasets, simply removing annotation artifacts will not solve the problem, as it creates other exploitable artifacts (Gururangan et al., 2018). Among the recent improvements in the dataset collection methodology are complex queries that require aggregating information from several sources (Dua et al., 2019; Kocisky et al., 2018; Yang et al., 2018). Reliance on shallow patterns could be reduced by paraphrasing, including adversarial paraphrasing with a model-in-the-loop as an oracle that would reject questions that were too easy (Dua et al., 2019). Another alternative is balanced datasets with as many question types and genres (Rogers et al., 2020). Diversity can also be somewhat improved with partly synthesized data (Labutov et al., 2018), but any templates or annotator examples themselves are potential sources of bias.

Questions are more difficult if they are collected independently from the text (Kwiatkowski et al., 2019), written from summaries (Trischler et al., 2016) or hints (Choi et al., 2018). Finally, unanswerable questions (Rajpurkar et al., 2018) in conjunction with adversarial inputs should also force the model to go beyond lexical pattern-patching.

A radically different direction is shifting to exclusively out-of-distribution evaluation (Linzen, 2020), e.g with adversarial (McCoy et al., 2019) and multi-dataset (Fisch et al., 2019) evaluation. However, for that we still need to be aware of the training distribution, which becomes particularly challenging because with very large pre-trained models it is hard to guarantee that the test examples were not seen in pre-training (Brown et al., 2020).

5 Diversity efforts

The tutorial will be presented by an all-female team with a senior researcher and a post-doc as the lead organizer.

The survey will focus on English datasets, but we will provide references to the existing datasets in other languages that we are aware of.

6 Organizers

Anna Rogers, University of Copenhagen arogers@sodas.ku.dk
Research interests: distributional and cognitive semantics, interpretability and evaluation of deep learning models, computational social science.
Organization: LREC T4 tutorial on compositionality in distributional semantics, CogALex-V Shared Task on the Corpus-Based Identification of Semantic Relations, the Third Workshop on Evaluating Vector Space Representations for NLP (NAACL 2019), the First Workshop on Insights from Negative Results in NLP (EMNLP 2020).

Anna Rumshisky, University of Massachusetts Lowell arum@cs.uml.edu
Research interests: distributional semantics, biomedical and social NLP, temporal reasoning, machine learning/deep learning for NLP
Organization: Program Chair for NAACL 2021, Organizer for LREC T4 tutorial on compositionality in distributional semantics, SemEval-2017 task 6 (#HashtagWars: Learning a Sense of Humor), Clinical Natural Language Processing Workshop at COLING 2016, NAACL 2019 and EMNLP 2020, SemEval-2019 task 11 (Normalization of Medical Concepts in Clinical Narrative), The Third Workshop on Evaluating Vector Space Representations for NLP (NAACL 2019), the First Workshop on Insights from Negative Results in NLP (EMNLP 2020).

References

Payal Bajaj, Daniel Campos, Nick Craswell, Li Deng, Jianfeng Gao, Xiaodong Liu, Rangan Majumder, Andrew McNamara, Bhaskar Mitra, Tri Nguyen, Mir Rosenberg, Xia Song, Alina Stoica, Saurabh Tiwary, and Tong Wang. 2016. MS MARCO: A Human Generated MAchine Reading COmprehension Dataset. *arXiv: 1611.09268 [cs].*

Collin F. Baker, Charles J. Fillmore, and John B. Lowe. 1998. The Berkeley Framenet project. In *Proceedings of the 17th International Conference on Computational Linguistics*, volume 1, pages 86–90.

Samuel R. Bowman, Gabor Angeli, Christopher Potts, and Christopher D. Manning. 2015. A large annotated corpus for learning natural language inference. In *Proceedings of the 2015 Conference on Empirical Methods in Natural Language Processing*, pages 632–642, Lisbon, Portugal, 17-21 September 2015.

Tom B. Brown, Benjamin Mann, Nick Ryder, Melanie Subbiah, Jared Kaplan, Prafulla Dhariwal, Arvind Neelakantan, Pranav Shyam, Girish Sastry, Amanda Askell, Sandhini Agarwal, Ariel Herbert-Voss, Gretchen Krueger, Tom Henighan, Rewon Child, Aditya Ramesh, Daniel M. Ziegler, Jeffrey Wu, Clemens Winter, Christopher Hesse, Mark Chen, Eric Sigler, Mateusz Litwin, Scott Gray, Benjamin Chess, Jack Clark, Christopher Berner, Sam McCandlish, Alec Radford, Ilya Sutskever, and Dario Amodei. 2020. Language Models are Few-Shot Learners. *arXiv:2005.14165 [cs]*, June.

Danqi Chen, Jason Bolton, and Christopher D. Manning. 2016. A Thorough Examination of the CNN/Daily Mail Reading Comprehension Task. In *Proceedings of the 54th Annual Meeting of the Association for Computational Linguistics (Volume 1: Long Papers)*, pages 2358–2367.

Eunsol Choi, He He, Mohit Iyyer, Mark Yatskar, Wen-tau Yih, Yejin Choi, Percy Liang, and Luke Zettlemoyer. 2018. QuAC: Question Answering in Context. In *Proceedings of the 2018 Conference on Empirical Methods in Natural Language Processing*, pages 2174–2184, Brussels, Belgium.

Matt Crane. 2018. Questionable Answers in Question Answering Research: Reproducibility and Variability of Published Results. *Transactions of the Association for Computational Linguistics*, 6:241–252.

Jacob Devlin, Ming-Wei Chang, Kenton Lee, and Kristina Toutanova. 2018. BERT: Pre-training of Deep Bidirectional Transformers for Language Understanding. *arXiv:1810.04805 [cs].*

Dheeru Dua, Yizhong Wang, Pradeep Dasigi, Gabriel Stanovsky, Sameer Singh, and Matt Gardner. 2019. DROP: A Reading Comprehension Benchmark Requiring Discrete Reasoning Over Paragraphs. In *Proceedings of the 2019 Conference of the North American Chapter of the Association for Computational Linguistics*, pages 2368–2378.

Myroslava Dzikovska, Rodney Nielsen, Chris Brew, Claudia Leacock, Danilo Giampiccolo, Luisa Bentivogli, Peter Clark, Ido Dagan, and Hoa Trang Dang. 2013. SemEval-2013 Task 7: The Joint Student Response Analysis and 8th Recognizing Textual Entailment Challenge. In *Second Joint Conference on Lexical and Computational Semantics (*SEM), Volume 2: Proceedings of the Seventh International Workshop on Semantic Evaluation (SemEval 2013)*, pages 263–274, Atlanta, Georgia, USA.

Adam Fisch, Alon Talmor, Robin Jia, Minjoon Seo, Eunsol Choi, and Danqi Chen. 2019. MRQA 2019 Shared Task: Evaluating Generalization in Reading Comprehension. In *Proceedings of the 2nd Workshop on Machine Reading for Question Answering*, pages 1–13, Hong Kong, China, November. Association for Computational Linguistics.

Mor Geva, Yoav Goldberg, and Jonathan Berant. 2019. Are We Modeling the Task or the Annotator? An Investigation of Annotator Bias in Natural Language Understanding Datasets. In *EMNLP*.

Max Glockner, Vered Shwartz, and Yoav Goldberg. 2018. Breaking NLI Systems with Sentences that Require Simple Lexical Inferences. In *Proceedings of the 56th Annual Meeting of the Association for Computational Linguistics (Volume 2: Short Papers)*, pages 650–655.

Suchin Gururangan, Swabha Swayamdipta, Omer Levy, Roy Schwartz, Samuel Bowman, and Noah A. Smith. 2018. Annotation Artifacts in Natural Language Inference Data. In *Proceedings of the 2018 Conference of the North American Chapter of the Association for Computational Linguistics: Human Language Technologies, Volume 2 (Short Papers)*, pages 107–112.

Robin Jia and Percy Liang. 2017. Adversarial Examples for Evaluating Reading Comprehension Systems. In *Proceedings of the 2017 Conference on Empirical Methods in Natural Language Processing*, pages 2021–2031.

Kelvin Jiang, Dekun Wu, and Hui Jiang. 2019. FreebaseQA: A New Factoid QA Data Set Matching Trivia-Style Question-Answer Pairs with Freebase. In *Proceedings of the 2019 Conference of the North American Chapter of the Association for Computational Linguistics*, pages 318–323.

Mandar Joshi, Eunsol Choi, Daniel Weld, and Luke Zettlemoyer. 2017. TriviaQA: A Large Scale Distantly Supervised Challenge Dataset for Reading Comprehension. In *Proceedings of the 55th Annual Meeting of the Association for Computational Linguistics (Volume 1: Long Papers)*, pages 1601–1611.

Tomas Kocisky, Jonathan Schwarz, Phil Blunsom, Chris Dyer, Karl Moritz Hermann, Gabor Melis, and Edward Grefenstette. 2018. The NarrativeQA Reading Comprehension Challenge. *Transactions of the Association for Computational Linguistics*, 6:317–328.

Tom Kwiatkowski, Jennimaria Palomaki, Olivia Redfield, Michael Collins, Ankur Parikh, Chris Alberti, Danielle Epstein, Illia Polosukhin, Matthew Kelcey, Jacob Devlin, Kenton Lee, Kristina N. Toutanova, Llion Jones, Ming-Wei Chang, Andrew Dai, Jakob Uszkoreit, Quoc Le, and Slav Petrov. 2019. Natural Questions: A Benchmark for Question Answering Research. *Transactions of the Association of Computational Linguistics.*

Igor Labutov, Bishan Yang, Anusha Prakash, and Amos Azaria. 2018. Multi-Relational Question Answering from Narratives: Machine Reading and Reasoning in Simulated Worlds. In *Proceedings of the 56th Annual Meeting of the Association for Computational Linguistics (Volume 1: Long Papers)*, pages 833–844, Melbourne, Australia.

Guokun Lai, Qizhe Xie, Hanxiao Liu, Yiming Yang, and Eduard Hovy. 2017. RACE: Large-scale ReAding Comprehension Dataset From Examinations. In *Proceedings of the 2017 Conference on Empirical Methods in Natural Language Processing*, pages 785–794.

Hector J Levesque, Ernest Davis, and Leora Morgenstern. 2012. The Winograd Schema Challenge. In *Proceedings of the Thirteenth International Conference on Principles of Knowledge Representation and Reasoning*, pages 552–561.

Tal Linzen. 2020. How Can We Accelerate Progress Towards Human-like Linguistic Generalization? *arXiv:2005.00955 [cs]*, May.

Bryan McCann, Nitish Shirish Keskar, Caiming Xiong, and Richard Socher. 2018. The Natural Language Decathlon: Multitask Learning as Question Answering. *arXiv:1806.08730 [cs, stat].*

Tom McCoy, Ellie Pavlick, and Tal Linzen. 2019. Right for the Wrong Reasons: Diagnosing Syntactic Heuristics in Natural Language Inference. In *Proceedings of the 57th Annual Meeting of the Association for Computational Linguistics*, pages 3428–3448, Florence, Italy.

Nasrin Mostafazadeh, Michael Roth, Nathanael Chambers, and Annie Louis. 2017. LSDSem 2017 Shared Task: The Story Cloze Test. In *Proceedings of the 2nd Workshop on Linking Models of Lexical, Sentential and Discourse-Level Semantics*, pages 46–51.

Timothy Niven and Hung-Yu Kao. 2019. Probing Neural Network Comprehension of Natural Language Arguments. In *Proceedings of the 57th Annual Meeting of the Association for Computational Linguistics*, pages 4658–4664, Florence, Italy.

Simon Ostermann, Michael Roth, Ashutosh Modi, Stefan Thater, and Manfred Pinkal. 2018. SemEval-2018 Task 11: Machine Comprehension Using Commonsense Knowledge. In *Proceedings of The 12th International Workshop on Semantic Evaluation*, pages 747–757, New Orleans, Louisiana.

Boyu Qiu, Xu Chen, Jungang Xu, and Yingfei Sun. 2019. A Survey on Neural Machine Reading Comprehension. *arXiv:1906.03824 [cs]*, June.

Pranav Rajpurkar, Jian Zhang, Konstantin Lopyrev, and Percy Liang. 2016. SQuAD: 100,000+ Questions for Machine Comprehension of Text. In *Proceedings of the 2016 Conference on Empirical Methods in Natural Language Processing*, pages 2383–2392.

Pranav Rajpurkar, Robin Jia, and Percy Liang. 2018. Know What You Don't Know: Unanswerable Questions for SQuAD. In *Proceedings of the 56th Annual Meeting of the Association for Computational Linguistics (Volume 2: Short Papers)*, pages 784–789, Melbourne, Australia.

Siva Reddy, Danqi Chen, and Christopher D. Manning. 2018. CoQA: A Conversational Question Answering Challenge. *arXiv:1808.07042 [cs]*.

Marco Tulio Ribeiro, Tongshuang Wu, Carlos Guestrin, and Sameer Singh. 2020. Beyond Accuracy: Behavioral Testing of NLP Models with CheckList. In *Proceedings of the 58th Annual Meeting of the Association for Computational Linguistics*, pages 4902–4912, Online, July. Association for Computational Linguistics.

Anna Rogers, Olga Kovaleva, Matthew Downey, and Anna Rumshisky. 2020. Getting Closer to AI Complete Question Answering: A Set of Prerequisite Real Tasks. In *Proceedings of the AAAI Conference on Artificial Intelligence*, pages 8722–8731.

Alexey Romanov and Chaitanya Shivade. 2018. Lessons from Natural Language Inference in the Clinical Domain. In *Proceedings of the 2018 Conference on Empirical Methods in Natural Language Processing*, pages 1586–1596.

Viktor Schlegel, Goran Nenadic, and Riza Batista-Navarro. 2020. Beyond Leaderboards: A survey of methods for revealing weaknesses in Natural Language Inference data and models. *arXiv:2005.14709 [cs]*, May.

Robert Speer, Joshua Chin, and Catherine Havasi. 2017. Conceptnet 5.5: An open multilingual graph of general knowledge. In *Thirty-First AAAI Conference on Artificial Intelligence*.

Shane Storks, Qiaozi Gao, and Joyce Y. Chai. 2019a. Commonsense Reasoning for Natural Language Understanding: A Survey of Benchmarks, Resources, and Approaches. *arXiv:1904.01172 [cs]*, April.

Shane Storks, Qiaozi Gao, and Joyce Y. Chai. 2019b. Recent Advances in Natural Language Inference: A Survey of Benchmarks, Resources, and Approaches. *arXiv:1904.01172 [cs]*, November.

Adam Trischler, Tong Wang, Xingdi Yuan, Justin Harris, Alessandro Sordoni, Philip Bachman, and Kaheer Suleman. 2016. NewsQA: A Machine Comprehension Dataset. *arXiv:1611.09830 [cs]*.

Eric Wallace, Shi Feng, Nikhil Kandpal, Matt Gardner, and Sameer Singh. 2019. Universal Adversarial Triggers for Attacking and Analyzing NLP. *EMNLP*.

Lilian D. A. Wanzare, Alessandra Zarcone, Stefan Thater, and Manfred Pinkal. 2016. DeScript : A Crowd-sourced Corpus for the Acquisition of High-Quality Script Knowledge. In *Language Resources and Evaluation Conference*, pages 3494–3501.

Aaron Steven White, Pushpendre Rastogi, Kevin Duh, and Benjamin Van Durme. 2017. Inference is Everything: Recasting Semantic Resources into a Unified Evaluation Framework. In *Proceedings of the Eighth International Joint Conference on Natural Language Processing (Volume 1: Long Papers)*, pages 996–1005, Taipei, Taiwan.

Adina Williams, Nikita Nangia, and Samuel R. Bowman. 2017. A Broad-Coverage Challenge Corpus for Sentence Understanding through Inference. In *Proceedings of the 2018 Conference of the North American Chapter of the Association for Computational Linguistics: Human Language Technologies, Volume 1 (Long Papers)*, pages 1112–1122, New Orleans, Louisiana.

Zhilin Yang, Peng Qi, Saizheng Zhang, Yoshua Bengio, William Cohen, Ruslan Salakhutdinov, and Christopher D. Manning. 2018. HotpotQA: A Dataset for Diverse, Explainable Multi-hop Question Answering. In *Proceedings of the 2018 Conference on Empirical Methods in Natural Language Processing*, pages 2369–2380, Brussels, Belgium.

Mark Yatskar. 2019. A Qualitative Comparison of CoQA, SQuAD 2.0 and QuAC. In *Proceedings of the 2019 Conference of the North American Chapter of the Association for Computational Linguistics*, pages 2318–2323.

Rowan Zellers, Yonatan Bisk, Roy Schwartz, and Yejin Choi. 2018. SWAG: A Large-Scale Adversarial Dataset for Grounded Commonsense Inference. In *Proceedings of the 2018 Conference on Empirical Methods in Natural Language Processing*, pages 93–104, Brussels, Belgium.

Sheng Zhang, Xiaodong Liu, Jingjing Liu, Jianfeng Gao, Kevin Duh, and Benjamin Van Durme. 2018. ReCoRD: Bridging the Gap between Human and Machine Commonsense Reading Comprehension. *arXiv:1810.12885 [cs]*.

A Crash Course in Automatic Grammatical Error Correction

Roman Grundkiewicz[†] and **Christopher Bryant**[‡] and **Mariano Felice**[‡]
[†] Microsoft / University of Edinburgh
[‡] ALTA Institute, University of Cambridge
rgrundki@inf.ed.ac.uk, {cjb255,mf501}@cl.cam.ac.uk

1 Motivation

Grammatical Error Correction (GEC) is the task of automatically detecting and correcting all types of errors in written text. Although most research has focused on correcting errors in the context of English as a Second Language (ESL) (Leacock et al., 2010), GEC can also be applied to other languages and native text. The main application of a GEC system is thus to assist humans with their writing.

Academic and commercial interest in GEC has grown significantly since the Helping Our Own (HOO) and Conference on Natural Language Learning (CoNLL) shared tasks in 2011-14 (Dale and Kilgarriff, 2011; Dale et al., 2012; Ng et al., 2013; Ng et al., 2014), and a record-breaking 24 teams took part in the recent Building Educational Applications (BEA) shared task (Bryant et al., 2019). Given this interest, and the recent shift towards neural approaches, we believe the time is right to offer a tutorial on GEC for researchers who may be new to the field or who are interested in the current state of the art and future challenges.

With this in mind, the main goal of this tutorial is not only to bring attendees up to speed with GEC in general, but also examine the development of neural-based GEC systems (Grundkiewicz et al., 2019; Choe et al., 2019a).

The tutorial will thus cover *introductory* material and near *cutting-edge* research.

2 Content

The tutorial will begin by introducing the task and describing some of its challenges in terms of the complexity of natural languages and technical limitations. For example, closed class errors, such as prepositions, are often easier to correct than open class errors, such as content words, because the confusion sets are smaller and they tend to require less semantic knowledge.

It will then continue by providing an overview of the evolution of approaches to the problem, including:

- Rule-based methods; e.g. Park et al. (1997), Schneider and McCoy (1998).
- Language model rescoring; e.g. Turner and Charniak (2007), Gamon et al. (2008).
- Error-type classifiers; e.g. De Felice and Pulman (2008), Tetreault et al. (2010), Rozovskaya and Roth (2011), Rozovskaya and Roth (2014).
- Statistical machine translation (SMT); e.g. Junczys-Dowmunt and Grundkiewicz (2016), Chollampatt and Ng (2017).
- Neural machine translation (NMT); e.g. Yuan and Briscoe (2016), Chollampatt and Ng (2018a), Junczys-Dowmunt et al. (2018), Zhao et al. (2019).

This will be followed by a review of GEC shared tasks for English, showing how they helped advance research in the field.

The next section will then introduce all English datasets available to GEC researchers, including the FCE (Yannakoudakis et al., 2011), Lang-8 (Mizumoto et al., 2011; Tajiri et al., 2012), NUCLE (Dahlmeier et al., 2013), JFLEG (Napoles et al., 2017) and W&I+LOCNESS (Bryant et al., 2019), and discuss challenges in annotation and corpus processing. It will also discuss standard evaluation procedures and metrics, including the M^2 Scorer (Dahlmeier and Ng, 2012), I-measure (Felice and Briscoe, 2015), GLEU

Proceedings of the 28th International Conference on Computational Linguistics: Tutorial Abstracts, pages 33–38
Barcelona, Spain (Online), December 12th, 2020.

(Napoles et al., 2016) and ERRANT (Bryant et al., 2017), and highlight their limitations (Grundkiewicz et al., 2015; Choshen and Abend, 2018; Chollampatt and Ng, 2018b).

After the break, the tutorial will continue by focusing on the development of state-of-the-art neural GEC systems (Grundkiewicz et al., 2019; Choe et al., 2019a). In particular, although SMT systems outperformed NMT systems for much of the past five years, a number of techniques, such as transfer learning from monolingual data, strong regularization, model ensembling, and using a large-scale language model, have closed this gap. We will also highlight the main challenges in neural GEC – data sparsity and sub-optimal decoding – and describe several proposed techniques to overcome them (Rei et al., 2017; Kasewa et al., 2018; Xie et al., 2018; Ge et al., 2018; Lichtarge et al., 2019; Grundkiewicz et al., 2019; Choe et al., 2019b; Chollampatt et al., 2019; Kiyono et al., 2019).

Finally, we will close the tutorial by discussing the findings of the BEA-2019 shared task (Bryant et al., 2019), and outlining future work and research directions. In particular, we will highlight the advent of low resource GEC, which strives to make it possible to build GEC systems for any language without human-annotated training data (cf. Bryant and Briscoe (2018), Stahlberg et al. (2019), Alikaniotis et al. (2019)).

3 Tutorial outline

A brief outline of the tutorial:

1. Introduction
   (a) Task definition
   (b) Linguistic and technical challenges
2. Historical approaches and shared tasks
   (a) Different approaches to error correction
   (b) Shared tasks on GEC
3. Data and evaluation
   (a) Annotation of error corpora
   (b) Artificial error generation
   (c) Evaluation procedures and metrics
   (d) Limitations of automatic and human evaluation
4. Neural GEC and current trends
   (a) GEC as a low-resource NMT task
   (b) Overcoming the data sparsity
   (c) Improving correction
   (d) Beyond the NMT approach
5. Recent and future work
   (a) Low resource GEC for other languages
   (b) Findings of the BEA-2019 shared task
   (c) Future directions

4 Prerequisites and reading list

A basic knowledge of machine learning (e.g. familiarity with precision, recall, F-score metrics, and ensemble methods) and neural approaches to natural language processing (e.g. the concept of sequence-to-sequence encoder-decoder neural models) will be helpful to understand the content of the tutorial.

Suggested reading list:

1. Automated grammatical error detection for language learners. Leacock, Chodorow, Gamon, and Tetreault (2010).

2. The CoNLL-2014 shared task on grammatical error correction. Ng, Wu, Briscoe, Hadiwinoto, Susanto, and Bryant (2014).

3. Building a state-of-the-art grammatical error correction system. Rozovskaya and Roth (2014).

4. Phrase-based machine translation is state-of-the-art for automatic grammatical error correction. Junczys-Dowmunt and Grundkiewicz (2016).

5. A multilayer convolutional encoder-decoder neural network for grammatical error correction. Chollampatt and Ng (2018).

6. Neural grammatical error correction systems with unsupervised pre-training on synthetic data. Grundkiewicz, Junczys-Dowmunt, and Heafield (2019).

7. An empirical study of incorporating pseudo data into grammatical error correction. Kiyono, Suzuki, Mita, Mizumoto, and Inui (2019).

5 Instructors

Roman Grundkiewicz is a Researcher at Microsoft Research and a Research Associate in the Institute for Language, Cognition and Computation at the University of Edinburgh. His research interests include machine translation and its applications to automatic grammatical error correction, automatic post-editing, and transliteration. He completed his PhD on "Algorithms for Automatic Grammatical Error Correction" at the Adam Mickiewicz University in Poznan, Poland. He participated in several shared tasks, winning the BEA shared task on GEC in 2019, and the WMT shared tasks on Automated Post-Editing in 2016 and 2018. His teaching experience includes courses on programming languages, artificial intelligence, natural language processing and machine learning. At the Machine Translation Marathons in 2018[1] and 2019[2] he ran tutorials on the Marian NMT toolkit[3] for an international audience.

Christopher Bryant[4] is a Research Associate in the ALTA Institute,[5] based in the Department of Computer Science and Technology at the University of Cambridge. His research interests include automatic grammatical error detection and correction, automatic corpus annotation, and computer aided language learning (CALL). He completed his PhD on "Automatic annotation for grammatical error correction" in 2019 and is the lead developer of the associated ERRor ANnotation Toolkit (ERRANT). Most recently, he also led the organisation of the BEA shared task on GEC in 2019, and has previously given a tutorial on GEC to an international audience at the first summer school on Machine Learning for Digital English Language Teaching in 2017.[6]

Mariano Felice[7] is a Research Associate in the ALTA Institute, based in the Department of Computer Science and Technology at the University of Cambridge. His research interests include grammatical error detection and correction, artificial error generation, automated generation of cloze tests and evaluation methods. He holds a PhD from the University of Cambridge, which focused on the generation of artificial errors to augment learner corpora for translation-based GEC. He was also one of the organisers of the BEA 2019 shared task on Grammatical Error Correction and a tutor of GEC at the first summer school on Machine Learning for Digital English Language Teaching in 2017.

[1] http://statmt.org/mtm18
[2] http://statmt.org/mtm19
[3] https://marian-nmt.github.io
[4] https://www.cl.cam.ac.uk/~cjb255/
[5] http://alta.cambridgeenglish.org/
[6] https://www.cl.cam.ac.uk/~hy260/ALTA-Summer-School-Chania-2017/
[7] https://www.cl.cam.ac.uk/~mf501/

References

Dimitris Alikaniotis, Vipul Raheja, and Joel Tetreault. 2019. The unreasonable effectiveness of transformer language models in grammatical error correction. In *Proceedings of the Fourteenth Workshop on Innovative Use of NLP for Building Educational Applications*, pages 127–133, Florence, Italy, August. Association for Computational Linguistics.

Christopher Bryant and Ted Briscoe. 2018. Language model based grammatical error correction without annotated training data. In *Proceedings of the Thirteenth Workshop on Innovative Use of NLP for Building Educational Applications*, pages 247–253, New Orleans, Louisiana, June. Association for Computational Linguistics.

Christopher Bryant, Mariano Felice, and Ted Briscoe. 2017. Automatic annotation and evaluation of error types for grammatical error correction. In *Proceedings of the 55th Annual Meeting of the Association for Computational Linguistics (Volume 1: Long Papers)*, pages 793–805, Vancouver, Canada. Association for Computational Linguistics.

Christopher Bryant, Mariano Felice, Øistein E. Andersen, and Ted Briscoe. 2019. The BEA-2019 shared task on grammatical error correction. In *Proceedings of the Fourteenth Workshop on Innovative Use of NLP for Building Educational Applications*, pages 52–75, Florence, Italy, August. Association for Computational Linguistics.

Yo Joong Choe, Jiyeon Ham, Kyubyong Park, and Yeoil Yoon. 2019a. A neural grammatical error correction system built on better pre-training and sequential transfer learning. In *Proceedings of the Fourteenth Workshop on Innovative Use of NLP for Building Educational Applications*, pages 213–227, Florence, Italy, August. Association for Computational Linguistics.

Yo Joong Choe, Jiyeon Ham, Kyubyong Park, and Yeoil Yoon. 2019b. A neural grammatical error correction system built on better pre-training and sequential transfer learning. In *Proceedings of the Fourteenth Workshop on Innovative Use of NLP for Building Educational Applications*, pages 213–227, Florence, Italy, August. Association for Computational Linguistics.

Shamil Chollampatt and Hwee Tou Ng. 2017. Connecting the dots: towards human-level grammatical error correction. In *Proceedings of the 12th Workshop on Innovative Use of NLP for Building Educational Applications*, pages 327–333, Copenhagen, Denmark, September. Association for Computational Linguistics.

Shamil Chollampatt and Hwee Tou Ng. 2018a. A multilayer convolutional encoder-decoder neural network for grammatical error correction. In *Proceedings of the Thirty-Second AAAI Conference on Artificial Intelligence*, February.

Shamil Chollampatt and Hwee Tou Ng. 2018b. A reassessment of reference-based grammatical error correction metrics. In *Proceedings of the 27th International Conference on Computational Linguistics*, pages 2730–2741, Santa Fe, New Mexico, USA, August. Association for Computational Linguistics.

Shamil Chollampatt, Weiqi Wang, and Hwee Tou Ng. 2019. Cross-sentence grammatical error correction. In *Proceedings of the 57th Annual Meeting of the Association for Computational Linguistics*, pages 435–445, Florence, Italy, July. Association for Computational Linguistics.

Leshem Choshen and Omri Abend. 2018. Automatic metric validation for grammatical error correction. In *Proceedings of the 56th Annual Meeting of the Association for Computational Linguistics (Volume 1: Long Papers)*, pages 1372–1382, Melbourne, Australia. Association for Computational Linguistics.

Daniel Dahlmeier and Hwee Tou Ng. 2012. Better evaluation for grammatical error correction. In *Proceedings of the 2012 Conference of the North American Chapter of the Association for Computational Linguistics: Human Language Technologies*, pages 568–572. Association for Computational Linguistics.

Daniel Dahlmeier, Hwee Tou Ng, and Siew Mei Wu. 2013. Building a large annotated corpus of learner English: The NUS corpus of learner English. In *Proceedings of the Eighth Workshop on Innovative Use of NLP for Building Educational Applications*, pages 22–31.

Robert Dale and Adam Kilgarriff. 2011. Helping our own: The HOO 2011 pilot shared task. In *Proceedings of the 13th European Workshop on Natural Language Generation*, pages 242–249, Nancy, France, September. Association for Computational Linguistics.

Robert Dale, Ilya Anisimoff, and George Narroway. 2012. HOO 2012: A report on the preposition and determiner error correction shared task. In *Proceedings of the Seventh Workshop on Building Educational Applications Using NLP*, pages 54–62, Montréal, Canada, June. Association for Computational Linguistics.

Rachele De Felice and Stephen G. Pulman. 2008. A classifier-based approach to preposition and determiner error correction in L2 english. In *Proceedings of the 22Nd International Conference on Computational Linguistics - Volume 1*, COLING '08, pages 169–176, Stroudsburg, PA, USA. Association for Computational Linguistics.

Mariano Felice and Ted Briscoe. 2015. Towards a standard evaluation method for grammatical error detection and correction. In *Proceedings of the 2015 Conference of the North American Chapter of the Association for Computational Linguistics: Human Language Technologies*, pages 578–587, Denver, Colorado, May. Association for Computational Linguistics.

Michael Gamon, Jianfeng Gao, Chris Brockett, Alexandre Klementiev, William B Dolan, Dmitriy Belenko, and Lucy Vanderwende. 2008. Using contextual speller techniques and language modeling for ESL error correction. In *IJCNLP*, volume 8.

Tao Ge, Furu Wei, and Ming Zhou. 2018. Reaching human-level performance in automatic grammatical error correction: An empirical study. Technical report, Microsoft Research Technical Report.

Roman Grundkiewicz, Marcin Junczys-Dowmunt, and Edward Gillian. 2015. Human evaluation of grammatical error correction systems. In *Proceedings of the 2015 Conference on Empirical Methods in Natural Language Processing*, pages 461–470, Lisbon, Portugal, September. Association for Computational Linguistics.

Roman Grundkiewicz, Marcin Junczys-Dowmunt, and Kenneth Heafield. 2019. Neural grammatical error correction systems with unsupervised pre-training on synthetic data. In *Proceedings of the Fourteenth Workshop on Innovative Use of NLP for Building Educational Applications*, pages 252–263, Florence, Italy, August. Association for Computational Linguistics.

Marcin Junczys-Dowmunt and Roman Grundkiewicz. 2016. Phrase-based machine translation is state-of-the-art for automatic grammatical error correction. In *Proceedings of the 2016 Conference on Empirical Methods in Natural Language Processing*, pages 1546–1556, Austin, Texas, November. Association for Computational Linguistics.

Marcin Junczys-Dowmunt, Roman Grundkiewicz, Shubha Guha, and Kenneth Heafield. 2018. Approaching neural grammatical error correction as a low-resource machine translation task. In *Proceedings of the 2018 Conference of the North American Chapter of the Association for Computational Linguistics: Human Language Technologies, Volume 1 (Long Papers)*, pages 595–606, New Orleans, Louisiana, June. Association for Computational Linguistics.

Sudhanshu Kasewa, Pontus Stenetorp, and Sebastian Riedel. 2018. Wronging a right: Generating better errors to improve grammatical error detection. In *Proceedings of the 2018 Conference on Empirical Methods in Natural Language Processing*, pages 4977–4983, Brussels, Belgium, October-November. Association for Computational Linguistics.

Shun Kiyono, Jun Suzuki, Masato Mita, Tomoya Mizumoto, and Kentaro Inui. 2019. An empirical study of incorporating pseudo data into grammatical error correction. In *Proceedings of the 2019 Conference on Empirical Methods in Natural Language Processing and the 9th International Joint Conference on Natural Language Processing (EMNLP-IJCNLP)*, pages 1236–1242, Hong Kong, China, November. Association for Computational Linguistics.

Claudia Leacock, Martin Chodorow, Michael Gamon, and Joel Tetreault. 2010. Automated grammatical error detection for language learners. *Synthesis lectures on human language technologies*, 3(1):1–134.

Jared Lichtarge, Christopher Alberti, Shankar Kumar, Noam Shazeer, Niki Parmar, and Simon Tong. 2019. Corpora generation for grammatical error correction. In *Proceedings of the 2018 Conference of the North American Chapter of the Association for Computational Linguistics: Human Language Technologies*, Minneapolis, USA, June. Association for Computational Linguistics.

Tomoya Mizumoto, Mamoru Komachi, Masaaki Nagata, and Yuji Matsumoto. 2011. Mining revision log of language learning SNS for automated japanese error correction of second language learners. In *The 5th International Joint Conference on Natural Language Processing*, pages 147–155.

Courtney Napoles, Keisuke Sakaguchi, Matt Post, and Joel Tetreault. 2016. GLEU without tuning. *arXiv preprint arXiv:1605.02592*.

Courtney Napoles, Keisuke Sakaguchi, and Joel Tetreault. 2017. JFLEG: A fluency corpus and benchmark for grammatical error correction. In *Proceedings of the 15th Conference of the European Chapter of the Association for Computational Linguistics: Volume 2, Short Papers*, pages 229–234, Valencia, Spain, April. Association for Computational Linguistics.

Hwee Tou Ng, Siew Mei Wu, Yuanbin Wu, Christian Hadiwinoto, and Joel Tetreault. 2013. The CoNLL-2013 shared task on grammatical error correction. In *Proceedings of the Seventeenth Conference on Computational Natural Language Learning: Shared Task*, pages 1–12, Sofia, Bulgaria, August. Association for Computational Linguistics.

Hwee Tou Ng, Siew Mei Wu, Ted Briscoe, Christian Hadiwinoto, Raymond Hendy Susanto, and Christopher Bryant. 2014. The CoNLL-2014 shared task on grammatical error correction. In *Proceedings of the Eighteenth Conference on Computational Natural Language Learning: Shared Task*, pages 1–14, Baltimore, Maryland, June. Association for Computational Linguistics.

Jong C Park, Martha Stone Palmer, and Clay Washburn. 1997. An english grammar checker as a writing aid for students of english as a second language. In *ANLP*, page 24.

Marek Rei, Mariano Felice, Zheng Yuan, and Ted Briscoe. 2017. Artificial error generation with machine translation and syntactic patterns. In *Proceedings of the 12th Workshop on Innovative Use of NLP for Building Educational Applications*, pages 287–292, Copenhagen, Denmark, September. Association for Computational Linguistics.

A. Rozovskaya and D. Roth. 2011. Algorithm selection and model adaptation for esl correction tasks. In *Association for Computational Linguistics*, Portland, Oregon, June. Association for Computational Linguistics.

A. Rozovskaya and D. Roth. 2014. Building a state-of-the-art grammatical error correction system. *Transactions of the Association for Computational Linguistics*.

David Schneider and Kathleen F. McCoy. 1998. Recognizing syntactic errors in the writing of second language learners. In *Proceedings of the 36th Annual Meeting of the Association for Computational Linguistics and 17th International Conference on Computational Linguistics - Volume 2*, ACL '98, pages 1198–1204. Association for Computational Linguistics.

Felix Stahlberg, Christopher Bryant, and Bill Byrne. 2019. Neural grammatical error correction with finite state transducers. In *Proceedings of the 2018 Conference of the North American Chapter of the Association for Computational Linguistics: Human Language Technologies*, Minneapolis, USA, June. Association for Computational Linguistics.

Toshikazu Tajiri, Mamoru Komachi, and Yuji Matsumoto. 2012. Tense and aspect error correction for ESL learners using global context. In *Proceedings of the 50th Annual Meeting of the Association for Computational Linguistics: Short Papers - Volume 2*, ACL '12, pages 198–202, Stroudsburg, PA, USA. Association for Computational Linguistics.

Joel Tetreault, Jennifer Foster, and Martin Chodorow. 2010. Using parse features for preposition selection and error detection. In *Proceedings of the ACL 2010 Conference Short Papers*, ACLShort '10, pages 353–358, Stroudsburg, PA, USA. Association for Computational Linguistics.

Jenine Turner and Eugene Charniak. 2007. Language modeling for determiner selection. In *Human Language Technologies 2007: The Conference of the North American Chapter of the Association for Computational Linguistics; Companion Volume, Short Papers*, NAACL-Short '07, pages 177–180. Association for Computational Linguistics.

Ziang Xie, Guillaume Genthial, Stanley Xie, Andrew Ng, and Dan Jurafsky. 2018. Noising and denoising natural language: Diverse backtranslation for grammar correction. In *Proceedings of the 2018 Conference of the North American Chapter of the Association for Computational Linguistics: Human Language Technologies, Volume 1 (Long Papers)*, pages 619–628, New Orleans, Louisiana, June. Association for Computational Linguistics.

Helen Yannakoudakis, Ted Briscoe, and Ben Medlock. 2011. A new dataset and method for automatically grading ESOL texts. In *Proceedings of the 49th Annual Meeting of the Association for Computational Linguistics: Human Language Technologies*, pages 180–189, Portland, Oregon, USA, June. Association for Computational Linguistics.

Zheng Yuan and Ted Briscoe. 2016. Grammatical error correction using neural machine translation. In *Proceedings of the 2016 Conference of the North American Chapter of the Association for Computational Linguistics: Human Language Technologies*, pages 380–386, San Diego, California, June. Association for Computational Linguistics.

Wei Zhao, Liang Wang, Kewei Shen, Ruoyu Jia, and Jingming Liu. 2019. Improving grammatical error correction via pre-training a copy-augmented architecture with unlabeled data. In *Proceedings of the 2019 Conference of the North American Chapter of the Association for Computational Linguistics: Human Language Technologies, Volume 1 (Long and Short Papers)*, pages 156–165, Minneapolis, Minnesota, June. Association for Computational Linguistics.

Endangered Languages meet Modern NLP

Antonios Anastasopoulos[†] **Christopher Cox**[◇] **Hilaria Cruz**[♣] **Graham Neubig**[‡]
[†]Department of Computer Science, George Mason University
[‡]Language Technologies Institute, Carnegie Mellon University
[◇]School of Linguistics and Language Studies, Carleton University
[♣]Comparative Humanities, University of Louisville
antonis@gmu.edu gneubig@cs.cmu.edu
christopher.cox@carleton.ca hilaria.cruz@louisville.edu

1 Description

Computational Linguistics and Natural Language Processing (NLP) have taken immense strides, spearheaded by neural methods and large data collections. The result is ubiquitous language technology and vast amounts of research on new tasks and products. However, the vast majority of the world's languages have been mostly ignored, including the most vulnerable among them: endangered languages.

The lack of communication between the NLP community and the documentary linguistics community is partly to blame (Bird, 2009). Even though field and documentary linguists produce resources and use NLP methods, this is done in isolation, as computational methods are seen as a means towards the final goal, which typically is language description. The extreme pace of language loss and the urgent needs for language revitalization, however, require that we utilize documentations and go beyond language description: enter 21st century NLP.

Himmelmann's 20-year-old radical vision (Himmelmann, 1998) for a data-centric approach to language documentation (which sparked the creation of modern documentary linguistics) has slowly begun to materialize (McDonnell et al., 2018). For example, the Workshops on the Use of Computational Methods in the Study of Endangered Languages (Comput-EL) (Good et al., 2014; Arppe et al., 2017; Arppe et al., 2019) have provided a small forum for the much-needed discussion between NLP practitioners and documentary and field linguists.

Meanwhile, increasingly more focus is dedicated on NLP research and bringing modern technologies to endangered languages. For example, mobile applications have been developed for data collection (Bird et al., 2014; Gauthier et al., 2016) and are actively used in documentation projects (Blachon et al., 2016); automatic speech recognition models have been created to aid with automatic phonetic or orthographic transcriptions focusing in indigenous Australian (Foley et al., 2018) or tonal languages from China and the Americas (Michaud et al., 2018); machine translation for under-represented languages have been presented as new corpora have been collected (Abbott and Martinus, 2018; Abate et al., 2018); cross-lingual transfer has been successfully applied for tagging, morphological analysis and inflection (McCarthy et al., 2019; Anastasopoulos and Neubig, 2019); multitask and active learning are being used for learning from continuous annotations on multiple tasks (Gerstenberger et al., 2017; Anastasopoulos et al., 2018; Chaudhary et al., 2019); approaches dedicated to indigenous polysynthetic languages have been developed (Schwartz et al., 2019; Kann et al., 2018); and computational methods have been used to study or discover typological features from large collections of text (Asgari and Schütze, 2017; Malaviya et al., 2017).

In this tutorial, we will outline the language documentation process and revitalization efforts, while also mapping them to concrete computational tasks. We will then focus on the machine learning approaches tailored to tackle these tasks under this very data-constrained setting. An overview of many of those NLP methods, as applied for language documentation, can be found in co-proposer Anastasopoulos' PhD dissertation (Anastasopoulos, 2019). Other surveys focus on the state of language technologies within specific geographic areas, such as co-proposer Cox's overview of Canadian languages (Littell et al., 2018) or the one by Mager et al. (2018), focusing on indigenous American languages.

The goal of our tutorial will be two-fold. On one hand, we will aim to acquaint the audience with the needs of the documentary linguistics community, and cover the already existing computational research

Proceedings of the 28th International Conference on Computational Linguistics: Tutorial Abstracts, pages 39–45
Barcelona, Spain (Online), December 12th, 2020.

in the field. On the other hand, we will discuss the capabilities and limitations of current computational approaches, so that the participants will know when and how to apply NLP methods, as well as how they could collect data and create corpora that can be used by NLP methods to aid both documentation and computational work. Ideally, by the end of our tutorial, the attendees will be familiar with the current research and the state-of-the-art in NLP for endangered language documentation and revitalization *and* be aware of the many standing challenges that lie ahead.

First, we will introduce the challenges posed by language documentation and revitalization, such as the transcription bottleneck, and how machine learning methods can fit into the pipeline. Unlike what is considered a typical NLP setting, working with endangered language data has intricate nuances: the lack of standard orthography, or even complete absence of a writing system; the extremely limited amount of data; language typologies widely different than anything used/tested in prior work; and even the lack of established benchmarks. We will discuss these nuances in depth, and how they relate or can be remedied with existing NLP research. We will also provide example code for many of these methods, and show how standard NLP pipelines need to be modified in order to account for these nuances. Finally, we will close our tutorial by discussing open problems and challenges.

Relevance to linguistics community This tutorial will bring together two linguistics communities, documentary/field linguists and NLP practitioners. As a result, we hope, the tutorial will *build enough capacity* of computational researchers that will be not only interested in NLP for endangered languages, but also aware of the current approaches and challenges. Elevating endangered languages NLP research is necessary towards bringing these under-represented communities to the spotlight, as speakers of such endangered languages frequently lack the skills to build NLP tools themselves.

Tutorial type The proposed tutorial combines the introductory and cutting-edge tutorial types. The acquaintance of computer scientists with the language documentation process will, by necessity, be at an introductory level. At the same time, though, the tutorial will cover cutting-edge NLP methods and their application to the endangered languages domain.

2 Tutorial Structure

The tutorial will be structured in order to be informative for both linguists (documentary, computational, or otherwise) and for computer scientists who are interested in performing computational work for language documentation and revitalization.

We aim for a three-hour tutorial that covers a reasonable range of all important aspects of this area. Times for the proposed structure are approximate, and they might be adjusted as we refine the tutorial content.

Part 1 [1h 20min]

- Introduction (45 minutes)
  - The language documentation process
  - The transcription bottleneck
  - The NLP tasks that are part of the documentation process
  - The NLP tasks that are necessary for revitalization
- When Data Assumptions Break (35 minutes)
  - The nuances of working with endangered language data
  - Code switching, code mixing, unstable orthographies and analyses, and how to deal with them
  - Creating corpora useful for both computational and linguistics research

Part 2 [1h 40min]

- NLP in extremely low-resource settings (40 minutes)
  - Speech Transcription
  - Tagging and other Annotation
  - Digitization and dictionary/grammar creation
- Multilingual/Polyglot models and cross-lingual transfer (30 minutes)
  - Using and choosing high-resource related languages

- Multilingual models
- Leveraging monolingual data and data augmentation

- Working with and addressing the needs of endangered language communities (20 minutes)
  - Community-centered documentation and revitalization
- Conclusion (10 minutes)
  - Resources for linguists
  - Resources for computer scientists

3 Recommended Reading List

The reading list is indicative of the multi-disciplinary coverage of this tutorial. We **highlight** the tutorial presenters in the papers they have co-authored:

1. Reflections on Language Documentation: 20 Years after Himmelmann 1998. Bradley McDonnell, Andrea L. Berez-Kroeker, and Gary Holton, editors. *Language Documentation and Conservation Special Publication No. 15*, University of Hawai'i at Manoa, 2018.

2. Challenges of language technologies for the indigenous languages of the Americas. Manuel Mager, Ximena Gutierrez-Vasques, Gerardo Sierra, Ivan Meza. *Proceedings of the 27th International Conference on Computational Linguistics: pp. 55–69*. 2018.

3. Natural Language Processing and linguistic fieldwork. Steven Bird. *Computational Linguistics: ed. 35(3) pp. 469–474*. 2009.

4. Deploying Technology to Save Endangered Languages. **Hilaria Cruz** and Joseph Waring. *preprint*, 2019.

5. Future Directions in Technological Support for Language Documentation. Daan van Esch, Ben Foley, and Nay San. In *Proceedings of the Workshop on Computational Methods for Endangered Languages* (Vol. 1, No. 1, p. 3). 2019.

6. Indigenous language technologies in Canada: Assessment, challenges, and successes. Patrick Littell, Anna Kazantseva, Roland Kuhn, Aidan Pine, Antti Arppe, **Christopher Cox**, and Marie-Odile Junker. In *Proceedings of the 27th International Conference on Computational Linguistics: pp. 2620–2632*. 2018.

7. Automatic speech recognition for under-resourced languages: A survey. Laurent Besacier, Etienne Barnard, Alexey Karpov, and Tanja Schultz. *Speech Communication 56*: pp. 85–100. 2014.

8. Integrating automatic transcription into the language documentation workflow: Experiments with Na data and the Persephone toolkit. Alexis Michaud, Oliver Adams, Trevor Anthony Cohn, **Graham Neubig**, and Séverine Guillaume. *Language Documentation and Conservation*: pp. 481-513. 2018.

9. Building Speech Recognition Systems for Language Documentation: The CoEDL Endangered Language Pipeline and Inference System (ELPIS). Ben Foley, Joshua T. Arnold, Rolando Coto-Solano, Gautier Durantin, T. Mark Ellison, Daan van Esch, Scott Heath et al. In *Proceedings of the 6th Intl. Workshop on Spoken Language Technologies for Under-Resourced Languages SLTU: pp. 205-209*. 2018.

10. Pushing the limits of low-resource morphological inflection. **Antonios Anastasopoulos** and **Graham Neubig**. In *Proceedings of the of the 2019 Conference on Empirical Methods in Natural Language Processing*. to appear.

4 Diversity Considerations

This tutorial has been constructed with a focus on encouraging diversity in all aspects:

- The content will aim to encourage diversity in Computational Linguistics and NLP, by promoting and encouraging research on the most under-represented group of languages: extremely low-resource and endangered ones.
- We will use real endangered language data for all examples, ranging from Mesoamerican languages to European dialects to indigenous languages of Asia.
- The instructors' team is fairly diverse both in terms of gender and in terms of seniority (one post-doctoral associate, three assistant professors). The presenters are affiliated with three different institutions from two different countries (from the US and Canada).

5 Prerequisites

- Machine Learning: a basic understanding of modern neural models.
- Programming and other tools: All code examples will be provided in Python, so knowledge of Python and basic command-line tools will be necessary in order to follow along.

6 Tutorial Presenters

Antonios Anastasopoulos is a Post-doctoral Associate at the Language Technologies Institute at Carnegie Mellon University. His interests include various aspects of multilingual Natural Language Processing and Machine Learning, with the main focus being Machine Translation and Speech Recognition for endangered languages and low-resource settings in general. He completed his Computer Science PhD at the University of Notre Dame, with a dissertation on *"Computational Tools for Endangered Language Documentation"*. He has been involved with documentation efforts on Griko, an endangered Greek dialect spoken in south Italy. He co-organized the workshop on Language Technology for Language Documentation and Revitalization, hosted in Pittsburgh in August 2019.
website: `http://www.cs.cmu.edu/~aanastas/`

Christopher Cox is an Assistant Professor in the School of Linguistics and Language Studies at Carleton University. His research centres on issues in language documentation, description, and revitalization, with a special focus on the creation and application of corpora representing Indigenous and minority languages. For the past twenty years, he has been involved with community-based language documentation, education, and revitalization efforts, most extensively in partnership with speakers of Plautdietsch, the traditional language of the Dutch-Russian Mennonites, and with Dene communities in western and northern Canada. He has served as an invited instructor in the area of language documentation and revitalization for community-based, national, and international events, delivering workshops for the Canadian Indigenous Languages and Literacy Development Institute (CILLDI), the Institute on Collaborative Language Research (CoLang), and the American Association for Corpus Linguistics (AACL), among others.
website: `https://carleton.ca/slals/people/cox-christopher/`

Hilaria Cruz is a field linguist with a focus on indigenous languages of Mexico, especially the Chatino languages (Otomanguean), which she speaks natively. She is also part of an interdisciplinary community of linguists and computer scientists who are working to create tools for automatic or semi-automatic transcription and analysis of audio and visual information for endangered languages. They have created a time-aligned speech corpus of transcribed, annotated with parts of speech, and translated Chatino data, which are available on an open-source basis. As a native person and field linguist, she has had many opportunities to teach linguistics in diverse settings and with diverse groups of students. She has taught general linguistics at the university level, in community organizations, and within Chatino communities. Her research interests include ASR for endangered languages, Chatino morphology, and promoting reading and writing in indigenous languages.

Graham Neubig is an assistant professor at Carnegie Mellon University specializing in natural language processing and machine learning. One of his major research interests is methods for low-resource language processing, and specifically for aiding the documentation of endangered languages. He has previously given well-attended tutorials at NLP conferences (EMNLP and NAACL) and the Lisbon and CIFAR Machine Learning Summer Schools. He has won a number of best papers at NLP venues (e.g. EMNLP2016, EACL2017, NAACL2019) and given a number of invited talks on the proposal topic of low-resource language processing, including at Google, UMass Amherst, and New York University.
website: `http://www.phontron.com/`

7 Details

Breadth We aim to provide the first wide coverage overview of NLP approaches for endangered languages. Out of the 25 referenced works (which is not an exhaustive list of the works we will cover) only 7 are co-authored by the presenters, and we expect only about 30% of the tutorial to be based on the presenters' prior work. Similarly, 60% of the suggested reading has not been co-authored by the presenters.

Audience Size Estimate The first three iterations of the Comput-EL workshops (which are very relevant to the theme of our tutorial) have been steadily growing in size, while a regional meet-up organized in Pittsburgh by co-presenters Anastasopoulos and Neubig drew about 40 participants. Similar tutorials on the use of NLP in the International Conference on Language Documentation and Conservation (ICLDC) also draw large crowds. Given this interest, we expect a healthy audience of at least 60 participants. To our knowledge, no similar tutorial has been given before at any NLP conference.

Technical Equipment Internet Access; the participants could bring their laptops in order to follow along with code examples.

Preferred Venues All venues are appropriate for this tutorial, and the presenters do not anticipate major conflicts.

Open Access We agree to the publication of our slides and a video recording of the tutorial. We will additionally make all other materials (complete reading list, software, example data) openly available online.

References

Solomon Teferra Abate, Michael Melese, Martha Yifiru Tachbelie, Million Meshesha, Solomon Atinafu, Wondwossen Mulugeta, Yaregal Assabie, Hafte Abera, Binyam Ephrem, Tewodros Abebe, et al. 2018. Parallel corpora for bi-directional statistical machine translation for seven Ethiopian language pairs. In *Proceedings of the First Workshop on Linguistic Resources for Natural Language Processing*, pages 83–90.

Jade Z Abbott and Laura Martinus. 2018. Towards neural machine translation for African languages. *arXiv preprint arXiv:1811.05467.*

Antonios Anastasopoulos and Graham Neubig. 2019. Pushing the limits of low-resource morphological inflection. In *Proc. EMNLP*, Hong Kong, November. to appear.

Antonios Anastasopoulos, Marika Lekakou, Josep Quer, Eleni Zimianiti, Justin DeBenedetto, and David Chiang. 2018. Part-of-speech tagging on an endangered language: a parallel Griko-Italian resource. In *Proc. COLING*, pages 2529–2539. Association for Computational Linguistics.

Antonios Anastasopoulos. 2019. *Computational Tools for Endangered Language Documentation*. Ph.D. thesis, University of Notre Dame du Lac, Notre Dame, Indiana, January.

Antti Arppe, Jeff Good, Mans Hulden, Jordan Lachler, Alexis Palmer, and Lane Schwartz. 2017. Proceedings of the 2nd workshop on the use of computational methods in the study of endangered languages. In *Proceedings of the 2nd Workshop on the Use of Computational Methods in the Study of Endangered Languages*.

Antti Arppe, Jeff Good, Mans Hulden, Jordan Lachler, Alexis Palmer, Lane Schwartz, and Miikka Silfverberg. 2019. Proceedings of the 3rd workshop on the use of computational methods in the study of endangered languages volume 1. In *Proceedings of the 3rd Workshop on the Use of Computational Methods in the Study of Endangered Languages Volume 1 (Papers)*.

Ehsaneddin Asgari and Hinrich Schütze. 2017. Past, present, future: A computational investigation of the typology of tense in 1000 languages. In *Proceedings of the 2017 Conference on Empirical Methods in Natural Language Processing*, pages 113–124, Copenhagen, Denmark, September. Association for Computational Linguistics.

Steven Bird, Florian R. Hanke, Oliver Adams, and Haejoong Lee. 2014. Aikuma: A mobile app for collaborative language documentation. In *Proc. of the 2014 Workshop on the Use of Computational Methods in the Study of Endangered Languages*.

Steven Bird. 2009. Natural Language Processing and linguistic fieldwork. *Computational Linguistics*, 35(3):469–474.

David Blachon, Elodie Gauthier, Laurent Besacier, Guy-Noël Kouarata, Martine Adda-Decker, and Annie Rialland. 2016. Parallel speech collection for under-resourced language studies using the LIG-Aikuma mobile device app. In *Proc. SLTU (Spoken Language Technologies for Under-Resourced Languages)*, volume 81.

Aditi Chaudhary, Jiateng Xie, Zaid Sheikh, Graham Neubig, and Jaime Carbonell. 2019. A little annotation does a lot of good: A study in bootstrapping low-resource named entity recognizers. In *Conference on Empirical Methods in Natural Language Processing (EMNLP)*, Hong Kong, November.

Ben Foley, Josh Arnold, Rolando Coto-Solano, Gautier Durantin, T. Mark Ellison, Daan van Esch, Scott Heath, Frantisek Kratochv'il, Zara Maxwell-Smith, David Nash, Ola Olsson, Mark Richards, Nay San, Hywel Stoakes, Nick Thieberger, and Janet Wiles. 2018. Building speech recognition systems for language documentation: The CoEDL Endangered Language Pipeline and Inference System (ELPIS). In *Proc. The 6th Intl. Workshop on Spoken Language Technologies for Under-Resourced Languages*, pages 200–204.

Elodie Gauthier, David Blachon, Laurent Besacier, Guy-Noel Kouarata, Martine Adda-Decker, Annie Rialland, Gilles Adda, and Grégoire Bachman. 2016. LIG-Aikuma: a mobile app to collect parallel speech for under-resourced language studies. In *Interspeech 2016 (short demo paper)*.

Ciprian Gerstenberger, Niko Partanen, Michael Rießler, and Joshua Wilbur. 2017. Instant annotations–applying NLP methods to the annotation of spoken language documentation corpora. In *Proceedings of the Third Workshop on Computational Linguistics for Uralic Languages*, pages 25–36.

Jeff Good, Julia Hirschberg, and Owen Rambow, editors. 2014. *Proceedings of the 2014 Workshop on the Use of Computational Methods in the Study of Endangered Languages*. Association for Computational Linguistics, Baltimore, Maryland, USA, June.

Nikolaus P Himmelmann. 1998. Documentary and descriptive linguistics.

Katharina Kann, Manuel Mager, Ivan Meza-Ruiz, and Hinrich Schütze. 2018. Fortification of neural morphological segmentation models for polysynthetic minimal-resource languages. *arXiv preprint arXiv:1804.06024*.

Patrick Littell, Anna Kazantseva, Roland Kuhn, Aidan Pine, Antti Arppe, Christopher Cox, and Marie-Odile Junker. 2018. Indigenous language technologies in Canada: Assessment, challenges, and successes. In *Proceedings of the 27th International Conference on Computational Linguistics*, pages 2620–2632.

Manuel Mager, Ximena Gutierrez-Vasques, Gerardo Sierra, and Ivan Meza-Ruiz. 2018. Challenges of language technologies for the indigenous languages of the Americas. In *Proceedings of the 27th International Conference on Computational Linguistics*, pages 55–69.

Chaitanya Malaviya, Graham Neubig, and Patrick Littell. 2017. Learning language representations for typology prediction. In *Conference on Empirical Methods in Natural Language Processing (EMNLP)*, Copenhagen, Denmark, September.

Arya D McCarthy, Ekaterina Vylomova, Shijie Wu, Chaitanya Malaviya, Lawrence Wolf-Sonkin, Garrett Nicolai, Christo Kirov, Miikka Silfverberg, Sebastian J Mielke, Jeffrey Heinz, et al. 2019. The SIGMORPHON 2019 shared task: Morphological analysis in context and cross-lingual transfer for inflection. In *Proceedings of the 16th Workshop on Computational Research in Phonetics, Phonology, and Morphology*, pages 229–244.

Bradley McDonnell, Andrea L. Berez-Kroeker, and Gary Holton, editors. 2018. *Reflections on Language Documentation: 20 Years after Himmelmann 1998*. Language Documentation and Conservation Special Publication No. 15, University of Hawai'i at Manoa.

Alexis Michaud, Oliver Adams, Trevor Anthony Cohn, Graham Neubig, and Séverine Guillaume. 2018. Integrating automatic transcription into the language documentation workflow: Experiments with Na data and the Persephone toolkit. *Language Documentation and Conservation*, pages 393–429.

Lane Schwartz, Emily Chen, Benjamin Hunt, and Sylvia LR Schreiner. 2019. Bootstrapping a neural morphological analyzer for St. Lawrence Island Yupik from a finite-state transducer. In *Proceedings of the Workshop on Computational Methods for Endangered Languages*, volume 1, page 12.